Elite • 215

British Light Infantry & Rifle Tactics of the Napoleonic Wars

PHILIP J. HAYTHORNTHWAITE ILLUSTRATED BY ADAM HOOK

Series editor Martin Windrow

First published in Great Britain in 2016 by Osprey Publishing
PO Box 883, Oxford, OX1 9PL, UK
1385 Broadway, 5th Floor, New York, NY 10018, USA
E-mail: info@ospreypublishing.com

Osprey Publishing, part of Bloomsbury Publishing Plc
© 2016 Osprey Publishing Ltd.

A CIP catalogue record for this book is available from the British Library

Print ISBN: 978 1 4728 1606 1
PDF ebook ISBN: 978 1 4728 1607 8
ePub ebook ISBN: 978 1 4728 1608 5

Editor: Martin Windrow
Index by Sandra Shotter
Typeset in Sabon and Myriad Pro
Originated by PDQ Media, Bungay, UK
Printed in China through Worldprint Ltd

16 17 18 19 20   10 9 8 7 6 5 4 3 2 1

Osprey Publishing supports the Woodland Trust, the UK's leading woodland conservation charity. Between 2014 and 2018 our donations will be spent on their Centenary Woods project in the UK.

www.ospreypublishing.com

AUTHOR'S NOTE

Two other Osprey titles can be consulted in conjunction with the present work: Elite 164, *British Napoleonic Infantry Tactics 1792–1815*; and Warrior 47, *British Rifleman 1797–1815*.

ACKNOWLEDGEMENTS

The author extends especial thanks to Derek Green, Dr John A. Hall, the late Edward Ryan, the late Dennis Sully, and Richard J. Tennant

ARTIST'S NOTE

Reader may care to note that the original paintings from which the colour plates in this book were prepared are available for private sale. All reproduction copyright whatsoever is retained by the Publisher. All enquiries should be addressed to:

Scorpio Paintings, 158 Mill Road, Hailsham, East Sussex BN27 2SH, UK
scorpiopaintings@btinternet.com

The Publishers regret that they can enter into no correspondence upon this matter.

CONTENTS

BRITISH LIGHT INFANTRY & RIFLE TACTICS OF THE NAPOLEONIC WARS

HISTORICAL BACKGROUND

The evolution of light infantry was arguably the most important tactical development of the mid- to late 18th century, and it laid the foundation for all the infantry service that followed.

Although there had always been lightly armed troops more suitable for reconnaissance and irregular warfare than the strictly disciplined 'heavy' or line infantry, this aspect of tactics began to develop more systematically

The architect: Sir John Moore (1761–1809), in the uniform of lieutenant-general, the rank he held when he was killed at Corunna. His central contribution to the development of the British light infantry was twofold: his insistence on an enlightened system of discipline that encouraged 'a new spirit which should make of the whole a living organism to replace a mechanical instrument'; and his understanding that such troops had to be capable of fighting either as 'Yager' or as 'firm battalions', according to tactical necessity. (Engraving by Charles Turner after Sir Thomas Lawrence)

during the middle years of the 18th century. To some extent it was initially the purview of specific irregular troops using what were then considered to be indigenous skills, for example the Croats and Pandours employed by the Austro-Hungarian armies; however, states lacking such distinct human resources within their territory had to convert 'ordinary' soldiers to this specialist role.

In the British Army, formally organized light troops came to some prominence during the Seven Years' War (1756–63). For cavalry reconnaissance duties a light troop was added to each of 11 dragoon and dragoon guard regiments in 1756, and light infantry came into being at the same time. Initially they were formed for specific campaigns in North America and Germany, to some extent in response to the terrain encountered – notably, the forested wilderness of America. Clothing and weaponry more suited to reconnaissance duties were introduced, such as small caps in place of cocked hats, and short-tailed coats sometimes stripped of decoration. Examples included the 80th Foot (Gage's Light Infantry), formed for service in America by Col the Hon Thomas Gage; this unit's uniform at one time included brown coats, and their arms were carbines or shortened muskets with browned or blued barrels to reduce tell-tale reflections. Similarly, the 119th Foot (Prince's Own) wore peaked helmets and red coats without skirts. Typically, both were disbanded at the conclusion of the war in 1763. (This is not the place for fuller details of British light infantry in North America, but interested readers will find material in Osprey Men-at-Arms 48, *Wolfe's Army*, and MAA 39, *The British Army in North America 1775–83*, both by the late Robin May and illustrated by Gerry Embleton.)

Some small degree of light infantry training persisted, however. For example, the 1768 Inspection Return of the 28th Foot noted that – by implication, unusually – the regiment had a light company which wore short coats and caps, although they also had 'proper' clothing like that of the other companies. Highland troops also seem to have been regarded as light infantry; for example, when in 1771 a board of general officers was convened to

'The Warley Heroes of the Light Infantry on Full March' – a caricature suggesting how light infantry at the training ground at Warley were viewed in c.1780. Note the 'trailed arms', the characteristic maned helmets with turned-up frontal flaps, and short jackets. (Print published by W. Humphrey)

5

Light infantry officer armed with a fusil, from a contemporary illustrated guide to the 'manual exercise'; he wears a Tarleton helmet and short-tailed jacket typical of the 1790s.

Marching Salute.

consider suitable light infantry equipment, it was recommended that the 42nd (Royal Highlanders) should continue to wear their existing uniform, but that their equipment should conform to that of the 'rest of the Light Infantry'.

These considerations were made necessary by the decision in 1770 that each battalion should have a light infantry company, which, together with the battalion's grenadiers, became known as the 'flank companies' (from their positions when the battalion was drawn up in line). This conversion was not universal: except for those on service in America, no light companies existed in the Foot Guards until 1793, when four were added to the 1st Foot Guards and two each to the 2nd and 3rd Guards. Although the value of light troops had been proven in America, where the terrain had made their use essential, the whole concept was so different from traditional practice – notably, in the idea that a light infantryman should be permitted to use his initiative – that it provoked great resistance from some of those in authority.

Such attitudes are exemplified by a comment by SgtMaj Patrick Gould, an old Guardsman, when drilling the Royal Edinburgh Volunteers (formed 1794): 'Steady, gentlemen, steady; a soldier is a mere machine. He must not move – he must not speak – and, as for thinking, no! no! – No man under the rank of a field-officer is allowed to think!'[1] (As many of those he drilled

1 Superior numbers in this text refer to the Source Notes on pages 61–63.

The enemy: an early French example of preceding an attack in column with a strong force of skirmishers, as became typical of French tactics. This depicts an action at Pérulle on 19 April 1793. (Print after Rochu)

were academics and lawyers, professionally accustomed to asking 'why?', it is small wonder that Gould remarked that he would rather drill five fools than one philosopher.)

These traditional attitudes were condemned by the small number of forward-thinking experts, such as George Hanger, an advocate of light infantry who served with Banastre Tarleton in America. In a pamphlet entitled *A Letter to the Right Honourable Lord Castlereagh* he stated: 'I hold in detestation and abhorrence all *Button* and *Buckle* officers whose minds... are confined to the drill and the parade, and extend no further; their whole thoughts are absorbed in the minutiae of discipline; their ideas soar no higher than pipe-clay, buttons, lacquering of caps, the precise length of the pigtail, even to a quarter of an inch.'

The French challenge in the 1790s

Partly as a consequence of such inbred conservatism, the skills of the light companies declined following the American War of Independence (1775–83), despite their oft-proven worth in those campaigns. This was especially unfortunate, since such abilities were needed urgently to combat the French system of tactics employed in the early campaigns of the Revolutionary Wars of the 1790s. Their practice of rapid attacks in column was to some degree the consequence of having to create large citizen armies with limited time for training; but the simultaneous employment of large numbers of light infantry who preceded such advances was a development of theories that existed prior to the Revolution, so French light troops were competent from the very beginning of what would develop into a 20-year world war.

Few European armies could counter the French *voltigeurs* effectively with light troops of their own, giving the French a crucial advantage. This was explained by Baron Gross in his treatise *Duties of an Officer in the Field and Principally of Light Troops* (London, 1801), which encapsulates the use of light infantry on the battlefield: 'The French, since the Revolution, have so

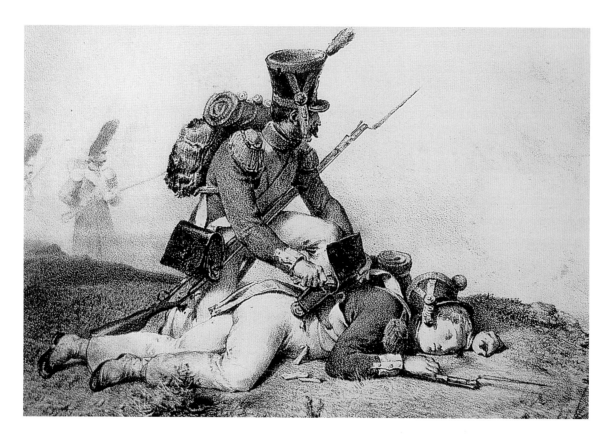

French light infantryman on the skirmish line, helping himself to cartridges from the pouch of a casualty.

successfully introduced such a new military system, that it becomes impossible to oppose them effectually, by any other mode than adopting one founded on similar principles. They send a number of riflemen in front of their line, to annoy their adversary, and conceal behind them the different movements of their columns; nothing can be effected against this disposition, but by opposing light troops to light troops.'

A comparison of French and British light infantry was made by John Money, who, unusually, had attained the rank of general in both British and French armies (in the latter, before Britain entered the Revolutionary Wars), and who thus saw these troops at close hand. In his *History of the Campaign*

A **SKIRMISHING**

This plate depicts skirmishers from the Light Division – 52nd Light Infantry and 95th Rifles – in the Peninsula, including some aspects of light infantry weapons-handling.

When skirmishing, light infantry always acted in pairs, with one member of the two always loaded and ready to fire, to protect his comrade. They were instructed to take advantage of natural cover and deliver aimed fire in their own time, not by volley. Light troops were trained to fire from the right side of whatever cover was protecting them and then withdraw to the left, to be replaced by the second man who would move forward and himself fire around the right of cover – a simple expedient that prevented the men colliding during the stress of combat.

The practice of loading under cover and only showing themselves to the enemy when firing was described by one

marksman as 'bo-peep' fashion. A technique mentioned at the time was the method of firing one-handed, in which a rifleman used his ramrod as a brace between the rear of the ramrod pipe and his waist belt, so that only the trigger-hand would be visible to the enemy. For firing prone, a number of contemporary illustrations show the use of the shako as a rest for the barrel (both these methods are illustrated at right). Another way to steady the barrel when aiming was to brace the loosened sling around the arm (centre).

(Inset) This depicts a sergeant of the 51st Light Infantry using his whistle to signal a movement order to his section of the skirmish line – a significant aspect of command-and-control in circumstances when verbal orders might be mistaken or not heard above the noise of battle.

of 1792 (London, 1794) he stated that in opposition to their French counterparts, British light infantry might line a hedge and poke their muskets through it, and (being trained to fire by platoon) would blaze away in the general direction of the Frenchmen's gunsmoke as long as the smoke lasted. Conversely, the French *chasseur* would take cover and only fire when he saw a clear target, and would usually hit it; he might fire only five or six shots in an hour, but with effect, while the British might fire 30 without doing any execution. He noted that the French generally deployed only one-third of their light troops while holding the remainder back as a supporting reserve – implying that this was not the British practice. Money also repeated a claim made elsewhere, that British officers were often moved from light to battalion companies just as they were beginning to learn their specialist duties.

The neglect of light infantry training in British service is perhaps exemplified by the fact that the infantry manual by Sir David Dundas, *Rules and Regulations for the Movements of His Majesty's Infantry*, established as the official system in 1792, devoted only nine pages out of 458 to light infantry. The consequence was, at best, that described by an officer present at the action near Alkmaar on 2 October 1799: 'Though perfectly unacquainted with the system of sharp-shooting (and it is impossible not to lament the want of that species of warfare in our army); though galled on all sides by offensive weapons that did their mischief, partly unseen, and always at a distance; though momentarily deprived of the encouraging presence of numbers of their officers, by the wounds they received; and although they themselves were neither equipped for light service, nor had the advantage of an advanced body for that purpose; notwithstanding this combination of unfavourable circumstances, our brave countrymen persevered and fought their way forward.'[2]

IMPROVEMENTS IN THE BRITISH SYSTEM

The *emigrés*

There had been, nevertheless, some attempts to regularize British light infantry training. Camps for the purpose had been held at Salisbury in 1774 and Goxheath in 1782, and in 1794 Sir George Grey, an early advocate of light troops, had established a school for light infantry in the West Indies. To compensate for the inexperience of British light infantry, however, a temporary expedient was the employment of Europeans, including some entire emigré corps, whose skills were believed to be more developed.

This practice extended to those officers entrusted with the development of light troops, of whom two were especially notable: Baron Gross, mentioned above, who was a field officer in the (British) Dutch Brigade; and Baron Francis de Rottenburg. Born in Danzig when that city was under Polish rule, Rottenburg served first in the French army; was seconded to Neapolitan service in 1787; commanded a battalion in Kosciuszko's Polish rebellion in 1791, and after its defeat joined Hompesch's Chasseurs in British service. In December 1797 he was appointed to command the 5th Battalion of the 60th (Royal American) Regiment – a unit largely German in composition, and the first regular rifle-armed battalion in British service.

Rottenburg's manual of 1797 was perhaps the most influential treatise on the subject, and was translated in 1798 as *Regulations for the Exercise of Riflemen and Light Infantry, and Instructions for their Conduct in the Field*. Its author was not named in the work; its introduction by the Adjutant-General William Fawcett (who may have made the translation) described him simply as 'a German Officer of Distinction'. Rottenburg seems to have been influenced by an earlier manual, *Abhandlung von dem Dienst der leichten Truppen* by the Hessian Oberst-Leutnant von Ewald, who had served in America (the Hessians being among the most expert light troops there), which was published in translation as *Treatise on the Duties of Light Troops* in 1803. Rottenburg's contribution did not end with his manual; in 1808 he instructed four battalions of light infantry at the Curragh in Ireland, and then trained three light regiments – the 68th, 71st, and 85th – at Brabourne Lees near Ashford in Kent. He led these, with two companies of the 2/95th, as a light brigade in the Walcheren expedition.

Another influential officer of foreign origin was Gen François Jarry de Vrigny de la Villette, a Frenchman who had served as an engineer in the Prussian army during the Seven Years' War, and had been head of the Prussian military college. He then served under Rochambeau and Luckner at the beginning of the French Revolutionary Wars, before emigrating in August 1792 to Britain, where he became inspector-general of the military colleges at Marlow and High Wycombe. His *Instruction concerning the Duties of Light Infantry in the Field* (London, 1803) played a considerable part in the development of British light infantry tactics, but he died in March 1807 before he could witness its effect.

Sir John Moore and the Perthshire Volunteers

Perhaps the most important single personality in the evolution of British light infantry was Sir John Moore, one of the most celebrated generals in British military annals. Several factors influenced this most far-sighted and liberal officer, not least his encounter with one of the army's newest regiments: the 90th Foot (Perthshire Volunteers), formed by the amateur soldier Sir Thomas Graham of Balgowan in 1794. Although not designated as light infantry until 1815, the 90th was trained in a form of light infantry exercise from its earliest days, as recounted by Col David Stewart of Garth of the 42nd:

'Major Kenneth Mackenzie, of the 90th... had practised this mode of discipline for several years, and while he commanded his regiment in Minorca, had brought the men to great perfection in it. One morning as he was at exercise on the Glacis of Fort St Phillips, General Moore, who was present, was so struck with its excellence and simplicity, that, with his usual openness and candour, he expressed great surprise that a thing so simple, and so admirably adapted to its purpose, had not before suggested itself to his mind.'[3] Moore had also been impressed by the light infantry drill practiced by Hudson Lowe's Corsican Rangers on that island in 1794, and the 90th had already been used as an example for officers' instruction by Sir Charles Stuart in Portugal.

From composite flank battalions to permanent light units

A significant organizational change was the extension of light infantry from the single company per battalion to larger units. The advantages had been recognized before Moore, exemplified by the temporary creation of composite light battalions by uniting the flank companies of a number of units. Larger light corps were potentially more effective than a

Thomas Grosvenor of the grenadier company of the 3rd Foot Guards, later a general officer. This shows the fusil carried by officers in the 1790s, when grenadiers appear sometimes to have been employed to supplement regimental light companies in the field. Grosvenor served with a Guards flank battalion in the Netherlands in 1793–94; he commanded the outposts in the Copenhagen campaign of 1807, and led the light troops in the expedition to Ferrol in 1809. (Print after John Hoppner)

number of individual companies, and in armies of limited size it increased the number of tactical units without materially weakening any of the component elements. For example, in 1776 a composite Foot Guards battalion was sent to America, reorganized subsequently into two battalions each including a grenadier and a light company, and these flank companies were usually detached to form a third battalion. Similarly, for the Netherlands campaign of 1793 the grenadier companies of three Foot Guards battalions were united to create a fourth, joined shortly afterwards by the new Guards light companies to form the Guards Flank Battalion; this process was repeated in the Netherlands in 1799. The inclusion of grenadiers in such formations at this early date implies that they were considered able to perform rudimentary light infantry service if required, perhaps exemplified by the fact that grenadier officers often carried light muskets.

The creation of such *ad hoc* flank or light battalions was so common that the system was even used in the organization of home-defence forces against the threatened French invasion. In the Yorkshire District, for example, in May 1798 a flank brigade was formed from the regiments stationed there, comprising one grenadier and one light battalion from the united flank companies of the 31st Foot, Nottinghamshire and Yorkshire Militias, and the 1st–3rd West Yorkshire Supplementary Militias (with a detachment of Royal Artillery added to each to crew the brigade's 'battalion guns'). Detached light companies might not even serve in the same campaign as the remainder of their battalions; for example, when the 8th, 12th, 33rd, 40th, 44th, and 55th Foot were serving in the Netherlands in 1794, the detached flank companies (their best elements) were with Grey in the West Indies. Composite battalions would also be employed in the Peninsula, as described below.

Characteristic light-infantry distinctions evident even in the auxiliary forces, here in the Birmingham Loyal Association in 1800: (left to right) men of the grenadier company, a battalion company, and the light company. The latter is the smallest and presumably the nimblest man, and wears a Tarleton helmet and short jacket. (Engraving by S.W. Fores after E. Rudge)

13

Among those who recognized the potential of larger units was one of the advocates of light infantry, Sir John Sinclair of Ulbster, colonel of the Rothsay and Caithness Fencibles. Sinclair proposed that four companies of each battalion should be converted to light infantry, and decried the idea that some men in every company should be trained to skirmish, by which 'you may lose the services of [the skirmishers] because the active may be of no use, being kept back by their sluggish companions; and unless they are previously divided into separate bodies, you cannot distinguish and separate them when they are wanted.'[4]

In 1799 it was decreed that the 52nd (Oxfordshire) Regt should form a 2nd Bn, of which Moore was appointed colonel-commandant, and upon the death in May 1801 of the regimental colonel, Cyrus Trapaud, Moore was appointed in his place. Among those who appreciated the need for proficient light troops was the Duke of York, the army's commander-in-chief, and according to Moore's brother the Duke consulted Sir John on the concept of creating regiments of riflemen:

'Moore observed, that our army was not so numerous as to admit of having enough of these for each detached force, which the nature of our warfare required. He therefore advised that some good regiments should be practiced as marksmen, with the usual muskets, and instructed both in light infantry manoeuvres, and also to act, when required, as a firm battalion. His Royal Highness approved this idea, and requested him to form his own regiment on that plan; and as many of the men were unfit for these complex duties, he was commanded to exchange them for more powerful and active soldiers, selected from both battalions.'[5] Moore had already expressed this opinion when training 12 battalion light companies and the 5/60th in Ireland in 1798–99: that unlike the light troops of some armies, 'Our Light Infantry... not only are employed as Yager [Jägers], but Act in Line... They are in fact a mixture of the Yager, and the Grenadier.'[6] This insight was to be of crucial

Deployment of light infantry: the order of march (right to left) of the British force that advanced upon Cape Town in 1795. The vanguard was provided by a composite grenadier battalion drawn from the regiments present; three battalions (1st & 2nd Seamen, and Marines) were formed from the fleet, and the artillery was escorted by seamen with pikes. The flanks were protected by detached light companies ('LC') in open order, supplemented by a company of seamen trained to fight in this way. Note that the '95th' Regiment present here was not the Rifle Corps but an earlier unit that briefly bore that number.

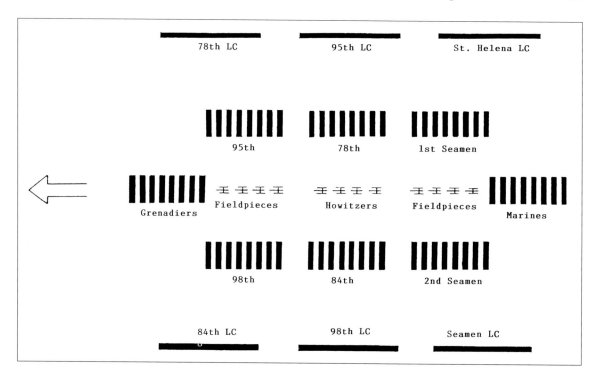

An early depiction of pairs of soldiers of the 95th Rifles, 1807. Note the powder horn strung on the single crossbelt supporting a pouch of prepared cartridges, the waist belt, and the long, straight sword-bayonet – the origin of the term 'sword' for bayonet in the rifle units ever since. (Print after J.A. Atkinson)

importance in the subsequent development of the British light infantry tactics. Consequently, on 10 January 1803 it was decreed that the 2/52nd was to be given an independent existence as the 96th Foot, and on 18 January that 'the 1st battalion, which will then become the entire 52nd Regiment, shall be formed into a corps of Light Infantry.'

The concept of light infantry able to act as line troops when required was also recommended by George Hanger in his pamphlet *A Plan for the Formation of a Corps which never has been raised in any Army in Europe* (1805). Such troops should possess 'the strength, solidity and force of fire of a regular battalion in close order; the activity, energy and rapidity in charge of British Light Infantry, acting either at open order or double open order... together with the destructive skill of a rifleman [and] act at such loose order as to imitate the subtle art of the Indian, who endeavours always to steal away the life of an enemy without exposing himself to danger.'[7]

To create his new 52nd (Oxfordshire) Light Infantry Regiment, Moore had Kenneth Mackenzie appointed as its commanding officer: 'an old, experienced, and skilful officer... generally considered the best commanding officer in the Army', according to George Napier. It seems that it was Mackenzie who perfected the tactical system rather than Moore; indeed, *The Royal Military Calendar* of 1820 stated that Mackenzie 'commenced with the 52nd a plan of movement and exercise, in which Sir John Moore, at first acquiesced with reluctance, the style of drill, march, and platoon exercise, being entirely new; but when he saw the effect of the whole, (he) became its warmest supporter'.

Moore's vision, and its success

However, Moore's contribution extended far beyond the mechanics of light infantry tactics, into the realm of a whole new ethos of military service. It involved a radical new concept that no longer regarded the ordinary soldier as a mere brick in the red wall, but saw him as an individual with an independent spirit; his initiative was to be prized and encouraged, by officers who were expertly trained and who regarded their subordinates as comrades. By the common attitudes of the day this was somewhat revolutionary, but Moore found enough other like-minded officers to put his theories into practice.

Moore was not alone in expressing these views; Dr Samuel Johnson had indeed suggested something vaguely similar a generation before, and the same was articulated by Robert Jackson, a regimental surgeon, physician, and sometime line officer. Widely experienced, and frequently at odds with the army's medical board (in 1807 he was sentenced to six months in King's Bench prison for assaulting the Surgeon-General in the street), Jackson nevertheless enjoyed the favour of the commander-in-chief, and his work of 1804, *A Systematical View of the Formation, Discipline, and Economy of*

B SKIRMISH LINE

The fairly typical skirmish-line illustrated (bottom) shows men of a company of the 52nd Light Infantry in the Peninsula, in two ranks 6 paces apart and in 'extended order', which officially left a lateral gap of 2 paces between each man, though this could be varied according to circumstance. Note that front and rear ranks are employing the 'covering' system favoured by the 52nd and 43rd: rather than the rear-rank men covering the gaps in the first rank, checkerboard-fashion, they stand directly behind those in the front rank, thus reducing by half the target visible to the enemy.

When the skirmish line was advancing, the rear-rank men moved forward around the front-rank men and 6 paces out in front of them, then fired. The new rear rank then moved forward similarly and, upon the signal that the other rank had reloaded, fired in their turn – and so on. In the 52nd and 43rd the front rank fired from a kneeling position: as the light infantry manual by the 'Very Humble Patriot' stated, 'the instant that the rank that is about to fire arrives at the ordered distance, it drops down to the kneeling position; in which it fires, loads, and waits until the signal to advance is again given. Thus no man is ever for a moment avoidably exposed'.

In the rear (top) of this scene, a supporting unit of Portuguese Caçadores advances at the double in column of twos, a standard mode of movement; the company will 'extend' into line when it reaches its allotted position. The Caçadores were an important element in the light infantry of Wellington's Peninsular army, and exemplified his description

of the Portuguese as 'the fighting cocks' of the army. Six battalions were formed in 1808, increased to 12 in 1811 by the formation of new units and the transfer from British service of the Loyal Lusitanian Legion. Usually a Caçadore battalion was combined with two line regiments to form a brigade. These Portuguese brigades were incorporated into Wellington's army at divisional level, though the 1st and 3rd Caçadores (and 17th Line) served seperately within the Light Division – the only Portuguese units integrated at brigade level.

(**Inset**) The Caçadores are shown advancing at the 'trail'. Cooper's manual stated that 'The arms in general are to be carried sloped, with bayonets fixed. Flanking and advancing parties may carry them trailed without bayonets, both for ease and for the purpose of taking cooler and more deliberate aim. In extended order, the arms are always trailed; in closing they should be shouldered and sloped'. The reason for aiming without fixed bayonets was to reduce the downward drag of the musket barrel, which could be unbalanced by the weight of the bayonet.

The Caçadores wore brown uniforms with various facing colours at collar and cuff. The headgear was initially the false-fronted *'barretina'* cap and subsequently this British 'stovepipe'. The uniform illustrated is that of the 3rd Caçadores, with the black facings they were allocated in July 1811. For fuller details see René Chartrand's Men-at-Arms 346, *The Portuguese Army of the Napoleonic Wars (2)*.

Armies, mirrored much of Moore's theory. However, perhaps the most important fact was that Moore was actually in a position to introduce this new system, which not only had a crucial effect upon training and light infantry tactics, but foreshadowed the nature of what might be considered as 'modern' infantry service.

Moore's theory was based upon the concept that 'each man had to work separately but in combination, [and thus] the essential thing required was not a new drill, but a new discipline, a new spirit which should make of the whole a living organism to replace a mechanical instrument'. In place of the traditional view of soldiers as mere automata, Moore insisted that officers should be trained thoroughly in pursuit of 'real knowledge, good temper, and kind treatment of the men', and that those men should look up to their officers and NCOs, who 'were to understand that it was their business to prevent rather than to *punish* crime'.[8]

Implicit in this concept was the encouragement of initiative on the part of the rank-and-file, which had a marked tactical application. It would enable even the lowest-ranking men to act effectively without supervision, founded on the confidence arising from thorough training. Relations between officers and other ranks were also much closer than in most regiments, and great encouragement was given to foster *esprit de corps* and the higher morale that it engendered, allied to self-confidence and comradeship. Several examples recounted by Charles Parker Ellis of the 1st Foot Guards confirm that these beneficial effects extended beyond the specialist units and into the light companies of conventional battalions. When Ellis's light company was engaged in heavy trench-digging in France in 1814, their general (presumably Peregrine Maitland) said that he would send some battalion companies to assist; but the light-company men went to their officer and 'said they hope his Honour would tell the General that they felt very grateful to him for his kindness, but that they had nothing to complain of... and that they would sooner work till they dropped down dead than have any d*****d Buffers [battalion-company men] amongst them, [so] the General very wisely left us to ourselves'.

Ellis recalled that during the same campaign 'some deserters gave information that the French intended to sortie that night; in going round the advanced sentries, I came upon a good old soldier, who was quite a character in his way; and on my telling him that he must be particularly vigilant and give immediate notice of any unusual sounds he might hear, he said, "I do not think that the French will come arter us, Sir." "Why so, Swinney?" asked I. "Why, sir, the last time as we had a brush with them, we sarved them up a sarce they did not much relish."[9]

An incident in Denmark in 1807, recounted by Rifleman Benjamin Harris, underlines the pride felt in the new units. Extended in a skirmish line, 'we now received orders to commence firing, and the rattling of the guns I shall not easily forget. I felt so much exhilarated that I could hardly keep back, and was checked by the Commander of the company (Capt Leech), who called to me by name to keep my place. About this time, my front-rank man, a tall fellow, named Jack Johnson, showed a disposition as though the firing had an effect on him, the reverse of what it had on many others of the company, for he seemed inclined to hang back, and once or twice turned round in my face... I swore by God that if he did not keep his ground, I would shoot him dead on the spot... During many years' arduous service, it is the only instance I remember of a British soldier endeavouring to hold back when his comrades were going forward. Indeed, Johnson was never again held in estimation amongst the Rifle Corps... Such was the contempt that he was held in by the Rifles, that he was soon afterwards removed from amongst us to a Veteran battalion.'[10]

A degree of independent spirit, without encouraging disobedience, had a significant effect on the tactical abilities of the light infantry. Coote Manningham, who was the first colonel of the 95th Rifles and who shared Moore's vision, described in his regimental regulations the ideal light infantry soldier as one who demonstrated 'the most peaceable conduct in his quarters, and the most generous courage in the field'. Perhaps an example of such a soldier was James Mansfield of the 45th, 'rather an awkward man [who] never was, in the strict sense of the word, a *smart* soldier. His uniform steadiness, and a conviction that he could always be relied upon, caused him to be placed in the light company, with which he served and made himself conspicuous for bravery.' Mortally wounded at Talavera, Mansfield begged to see his captain, Leonard Greenwell, and asked 'My hour is come... have I done my duty as a good and brave soldier?' 'Most undoubtedly... like an excellent one.' 'Well then, I die happy and contented.' As Greenwell observed, 'It was the spirit of Abercrombie in the humblest rank of the army.'[11]

Certain inherent characteristics or occupations might also have contributed to producing an efficient light infantryman, even in the auxiliary forces. For example, the light company of the North Pevensey Legion in Kent was composed of poachers and smugglers whose civilian skills would have been of great value in skirmishing warfare. (Nevertheless, it was stated that it was necessary to keep them so busy with training that 'they may not take a worse course', and that they paraded away from the rest of the unit so as not to embarass the upright men who comprised it.)

A typical rifle corps uniform based on that of the 95th: the green-clad rifle company of the 6th Loyal London Volunteers, 1804, showing the 'rifle' equipment – powder horn and priming flask, waist belt, and sword-bayonet. (Print by and after P.W. Tompkins, published by Elizabeth Walker)

The regiments

Moore's system had an immediate effect: as early as 1804, in his open letter to William Pitt, the experienced Sir Robert Wilson noted that the 52nd was 'indisputedly one of the first corps in the Service in every respect. The cat-o'-nine-tails is never used, and yet discipline is there seen in the highest state of perfection.'[12] It was not, however, the first entire regiment to be constituted officially as light infantry. In 1800 an Experimental Corps of Riflemen had been formed, which on 25 December 1802 became the 95th Rifle Corps; its colonel

The uniform of 1800–12, worn by a private and officer of the light company of a line regiment – here, one of the red-coated non-rifle battalions of the 60th (Royal American) Regiment. This shows the original heavy leather shako with the light-infantry distinctions of a green tuft and a bugle-horn badge, and the breeches and long gaiters of barracks dress. (Print after P.W. Reynolds)

was Coote Manningham, ex-41st Foot, a leading exponent of light infantry tactics which he had practised in the West Indies. (For further details of the rifle corps in particular, see Osprey Warrior 47, *British Rifleman 1797–1815*.)

In addition to the 95th – which ultimately comprised three battalions, and was to become a cornerstone of the army in the Peninsula – there was already one entirely rifle-armed unit: the 5th Bn, 60th (Royal American) Regiment. This was formed in December 1799 with personnel from previous 'foreign corps', including Löwenstein's Chasseurs and Fusiliers and Hompesch's Chasseurs and Fusiliers, who were already trained in light infantry style. (See

Officer and private of 85th (Bucks Volunteers) Light Infantry, 1809; the shako is now the lighter felt pattern. Note that both these prints show the officers' 'metal' as silver and the privates' as brass. Together with the 'wings' on the jacket shoulders, characteristic light infantry features are the officer's corded sash, and his sabre carried on slings. (Print after P.W. Reynolds)

René Chartrand's MAA 328, *Emigré & Foreign Troops in British Service (1): 1793–1802*.) Other green-uniformed rifle companies were added to the 60th's four red-coated battalions, and a 6th Bn was added in 1799 with an integral rifle company. In 1813 the 7th and 8th Bns were formed, each with two rifle companies and apparently with the whole battalions clad in green. In December 1815 the entire regiment was finally ordered to adopt green uniforms, although the 5th Bn was still the only one armed exclusively with rifles.

The next regiment to be converted to light infantry was the 43rd (Monmouthshire) Regt, on 17 July 1803; their light company had already

Details of an officer's version of the small cap worn by light infantry prior to the introduction of the 1800 'stovepipe' shako: the embroidered front panel, and low rear headband with the 'LI' of a battalion's light infantry company. (Courtesy Dr J.A. Hall)

been trained under Grey in the West Indies. Other regiments followed: in 1808, the 68th (Durham) and 85th (Bucks Volunteers) became light infantry, and in 1809 the 51st (2nd Yorkshire West Riding) and 71st (Glasgow Highland) Regiments.

Such was the significance that light infantry attained that a number of militia regiments were similarly converted, beginning with the lst–3rd Guernsey in 1804 and the Sark apparently from 1805. Many others followed from 1809, three of which subsequently became rifle corps (Royal Pembroke, Royal Flintshire and Royal Denbigh, in 1811, 1812, and 1813 respectively). There were also some specialist light troops among the ordinary militia regiments; for example, from 1795 the North York Militia had two companies of 'light armed marksmen' dressed in green, and the Sussex Militia included a green-clad rifle company c.1803. Although the North York companies may not have been armed with rifles until as late as 1805, their initial equipment included items traditionally associated with light infantry such as hatchets and waterproof gun-cases. Numbers of local volunteer corps were trained as light infantry, and some commentators advocated that the entire force be so classified. These included Robert Craufurd, and John Money, who declared that 24 days' drill would not produce troops equal to those of the line, but a competent sharpshooter could be produced in ten days, and it was as sharpshooters that the local volunteers would have been most effective in opposing the threatened French invasion.

UNIFORMS & WEAPONS

Conforming to Moore's concept of light troops being also 'firm battalions', there was never any attempt to clothe light infantry units in a different colour from that of the ordinary infantry, like the dark green of the rifle corps. This was despite an experiment conducted by Charles Hamilton Smith in 1800. Using a rifle company of the 6/60th recently returned from the Netherlands campaign (in which they had worn grey Austrian Jäger uniform), he had them fire at grey, green, and red targets. The last of these was shot to pieces, the green less so, and the grey proved the most difficult to hit; nevertheless, grey uniforms were never introduced.

Within the confines of the ordinary infantry uniform, however, there were characteristic distinctions especially suitable for light infantry service. Most notable was the use of short-tailed jackets, more convenient for skirmishing than the long-tailed coats of the line, who themselves adopted the shortened pattern in 1801 (officers in 1812). Headgear also marked the light infantryman, especially prior to 1800; the cocked hat had long proved unsuitable for skirmishing and rapid movement, and light troops adopted small, close-fitting caps. Unlike the simple 'jockey caps' cut down from tricorns in North America during the Seven Years' War, these would become increasingly decorative, with the addition of features like raised combs with horsehair manes, and elaborate badges, such as the St George and Dragon device of the 5th Foot and the Britannia of the 9th. It was complained that these caps had become as much for show as practicality; they were too small, and (as remarked in the 1791 Inspection Return of the 30th Foot), they lacked the shade for the eyes that aided aiming. Rather more practical were the brimmed 'round hats' used on campaign in the American War of Independence and subsequently – for example, by the Guards light companies in the 1790s.

Like the line infantry, from 1800 the light troops adopted the 'stovepipe' shako, albeit with a bugle-horn badge less likely to reflect sunlight than the large brass plate. Officers also adopted the shako (line officers retained their bicorns until 1812), and officers of light companies in line regiments used the shako as well, sometimes with distinctive features, such as the green lower band and gilt thistle device of the 91st. Green plumes were so distinctive of light infantry that Charles Parker Ellis of the 1st Foot Guards adopted the *nom-de-plume* 'Green Feather' for his Peninsular reminiscences.

Some distinctions in uniform were maintained for reasons of *esprit de corps* rather than utility (such as the shoulder-wings of the flank companies), and among critics of such features was John Patterson of the 50th. He wrote that 'the light bob took a pride in all that sort of thing [and] so much was our dress committee affected by the "scarlet mania" that red jackets could not be dispensed with... the glaring colour of their uniform almost neutralized the efforts of our gallant flankers... thus attired, they were but decked as victims for the slaughter.'[13] Other light infantry distinctions were probably more practical, such as their short calf-length gaiters. Their equipment was generally like that of the line, and some practical recommendations seem not

LEFT A typical early light infantry company uniform, emphasizing its relative practicality: small cap, short jacket, and short gaiters. (Engraving by F.D.Soiron after Henry Bunbury, 1791)

RIGHT Portrait silhouette of an officer of a regimental light company, *c.*1800, wearing the Tarleton light dragoon helmet that exemplified the use of light cavalry styles by the light infantry. This example has a flamboyant chained or corded turban and a large green feather plume.

This portrait of Capt Englebert Lutyens of the 20th (East Devon) Regiment shows the light infantry company's bugle-horn device and laced shoulder wing. A veteran of the Peninsula, Lutyens later served as orderly officer to Napoleon's household on St Helena.

LEFT An alternative to the laced wing that distinguished light infantry company officers: some regiments used chain-covered wings, which afforded some protection against sword-cuts.

RIGHT Officer's epaulette of a light infantry regiment, showing the bugle-horn device.

to have been adopted; one such was the suggestion by the board of general officers in 1771 that in wartime light troops should be provided with a 'maude' (a Scottish plaid) instead of a blanket.

Attempts were made to provide the light infantry with the most suitable firearm, including lighter muskets sometimes styled 'fusils' or 'fuzees'. In April 1769 sergeants of grenadier companies had been instructed to carry light fusils or carbines; the use of similar weapons spread to officers, and not just those of flank companies. As early as 1768, for example, the Inspection Return of the 15th Foot noted that all officers carried 'fuzees', and in July 1770 it was ordered that they were to be used by all officers of fusilier regiments. An example of such weapons was quoted in an official Ordnance list of 1794, which listed a 'Serjeants Carbine' with a 39in barrel and carbine bore, as against the 42in barrel and musket bore of the current 'Short Land Musquet'.

The use of firearms by officers declined; for example, in May 1792 it was ordered that they be discontinued by regiments serving in Ireland, but that sergeants of light infantry should keep their fusils – evidence that the order concerning grenadier sergeants had sensibly been extended to light companies. In the Napoleonic Wars few officers, even of light corps, carried firearms; for example, when Lt John Fitzmaurice of the 95th claimed to have fired the first British shot at Quatre Bras he had to borrow a rifle from one of his men to do so. A few officers did carry firearms on their own initiative, like the crack rifle shot Lt Joseph Owgan of the 88th (who on one occasion almost shot his own captain, William Seton, who was returning from a single-handed reconnaissance, crawling through tall heathland scrub on all fours).

Although regimental light companies probably used the ordinary musket, a special weapon was designed for the light regiments. In June 1803 a 'fuzee' was ordered for the 52nd and others, fitted with a notched backsight to aid aiming, a browned barrel (so as not to give away positions by reflecting light), and a canvas cover to protect the lock. The pressure on manufacture caused by the renewal of the war seems to have delayed its introduction, but by 1810 about 10 per cent of the muskets manufactured were of the light infantry pattern, each costing a shilling more than the standard 'Brown Bess'. It had a 39in barrel, and a scrolled trigger guard providing a pistol-grip as an aid to aiming; it subsequently received a lighter lock only 6in long, an inch

LEFT Rare example of the light infantry bugle-horn and the king's reversed 'GR' cypher on an officer's waist belt clasp.

RIGHT Light infantry sometimes used distinctive equipment. This brass slider from a black leather bayonet crossbelt bears the bugle-horn and the initials of the Royal Carmarthen Fusiliers, which became light infantry in 1803.

shorter than the ordinary musket. It seems to have been an effective weapon: Lt G.B. Jackson of the 43rd wrote that the muskets carried by his regiment and the 52nd in the Peninsula 'were of rather a superior description to that in general use at the time, and *greatly superior* to those with which the French troops were armed'.[14]

During the American War of Independence light infantry had been equipped with powder horns, but evidently the use of ordinary prepared cartridges became so universal that in 1784 it was stated that as horns and bullet bags were used so rarely, they should be discontinued. Flasks were retained by the rifle corps (which also used prepared cartridges) for their Baker rifles, a weapon capable of extraordinary feats of marksmanship in the hands of a trained sharpshooter.

Flank company officers usually carried sabres, presumably believing them to be handier than the straight-bladed weapon standardized for infantry officers in 1786. The pattern of curved sabre was unregulated until 1803, but even after the introduction of the official pattern regimental variations persisted, notably the stirrup hilt used by the 52nd. The regulation weapon was not admired universally: John Kincaid of the 95th condemned it as the 'small regulation half-moon sabre, better calculated to shave a lady's maid than a Frenchman's head'.[15] Sir John Moore expressed a preference for 'a straight sword, sharp on both edges', remarking that one had saved his life in Corsica when he had to run through a French grenadier who attacked him with a bayonet, which he could not have done with a curved blade (although 'he should never forget the horrid sensation it gave him when drawing the sword out of the man's body').[16]

INSTRUCTION

Discipline

The inculcation of discipline among light infantry, who might operate away from the immediate supervision of their superiors, was clearly even more important than in the infantry in general. It was founded upon Moore's concept of humane treatment, and the notion that officers and rank-and-file were all comrades despite the gulf in social status. Coote Manningham's regulations for the 95th noted that 'real discipline implies obedience and

respect whenever it is due on the one hand, and on the other a just but energetic use of command and responsibility'. Many officers of light troops exemplified this ideal, such as Sir Andrew Barnard of the 95th, of whom his comrade Jonathan Leach wrote: 'For a thorough knowledge of their profession, calm, cool courage, great presence of mind in action, frank and gentlemanly manners, and the total absence of what may be termed teazing [sic] those under their command, both Baron Alten and Colonel Barnard merited the high estimation in which they were held.' [17]

Even officers such as these resorted to the harsh punishments of the day when necessary, but could nevertheless be respected. Robert Craufurd, the legendary commander of the Light Division in the Peninsula, was known for draconian discipline, but was still worshipped by men like Benjamin Harris, who thought him 'the very picture of a warrior. I shall never forget Craufurd if I live to a hundred years. He was in everything a soldier... if he flogged two, he saved hundreds from death... he seemed an iron man; nothing daunted him – nothing turned him from his purpose. War was his very element, and toil and danger seemed to call forth only an increasing determination to surmount them.' [18]

Coote Manningham, first colonel of the 95th Rifles, whose uniform he wears. He died as a major-general following the privations of the retreat to Corunna in 1809. His regimental orders were very advanced for the time, and exemplified the light-infantry ethos cultivated by Moore and his colleagues. His public lectures, derived from the work of Baron Gross, were a model for the conduct of outpost duty (see main text, pages 44–45.)

Manningham's system of discipline was founded on the principle that officers should understand their men and know their characters, and should treat them equally and fairly, this being 'the best plan for maintaining discipline; this mode prevents evil being done, and all preventions are worth ten corrections'. All orders, from officers or NCOs, were to be given in 'the language of moderation [and with] regard to the feelings of the individual... abuse, bad language or blows, being positively forbid'. Salutes were only to be given to officers and the sergeant-major, not to NCOs. All were encouraged to attend the regimental school; indeed, all sergeants had to be literate and to understand arithmetic. The consequence of this enlightened system was an enhancement of morale, *esprit de corps*, and self-confidence which had a marked effect on those dispersed in the skirmish line. The important tactical author, MajGen J.F.C., Fuller, wrote in 1924 that Manningham's orders, based on comradeship, humanity, and common sense, were as relevant in Fuller's day as when they were written, and that no similar orders, 'ancient or modern... can rival, let alone equal, them [and they are] in every respect worthy to be copied.' [19] Spreading through the light infantry, such attitudes would come to set the template for all subsequent military service.

Training

Sir George Murray stated that Moore told him that his idea was not to create a new form of infantry, but to introduce a faster and less formal system of manoeuvre than that prescribed in Dundas's regulations. The

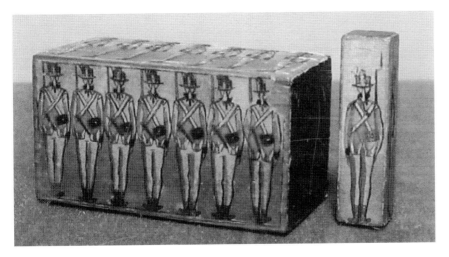

Light infantry distinctions were so well recognized that they even featured in the illustrations of this officers' instructional tool – 'West's Military Figures for the Practice of Tacticks' [sic], originally issued in 1797. Each company and marker sergeant was represented by an illustrated wooden block, used to explain and practise the standard manoeuvres. Battalion companies were shown in the conventional cocked hat and long-tailed coat, but the light company in a fur-crested 'round hat', short jacket, and light infantry 'pantaloons'. (Courtesy R.J. Tennant)

increase of speed and flexibility of formation produced what George Gawler of the 52nd described as 'pliable solidarity'.[20] Moore envisaged that men so trained would retain all the capabilities of ordinary infantry but with an added dimension.

Rottenburg's official manual was not the only guide for light infantry training; a number of others were produced, some of which had a considerable influence. A notable production of 1804 was *Instructions for the Formation and Exercise of Volunteer Sharp-Shooters* by the artist John Thomas Barber Beaumont, commandant of the Duke of Cumberland's Sharpshooters, a corps noted for 'the vivacity of the movements' according to Henry Angelo's

Rear Rank Firing

Center Rank Firing

Light infantry depicted in a guide to the 'manual exercise' demonstrating the pose for firing, including such subtleties as the rear rank (left) having the body angled rather more forward than the upright pose for the centre or front rank (right).

Reminiscences... (London, 1904). An influential manual of 1806 was *A Practical Guide for the Light Infantry Officer* by Capt Thomas H. Cooper of the 56th, which included remarkably clear diagrams. Published in 1809 but known earlier was *Instructions for Light Infantry and Riflemen* by Col Neil Campbell of Duntroon; perhaps best remembered as the British commissioner during Napoleon's sojourn on Elba, Campbell was a friend of Moore who had served in the 95th and 43rd, and who led the 16th Portuguese in the Peninsula. Another manual by a light infantry expert, published in 1823 but based on earlier practice, was *A System of Drill and Manoeuvres as Practised in the 52nd Light Infantry* by Capt John Cross of that regiment, who had served throughout the Peninsula (including ten major actions from Corunna to Toulouse) and at Waterloo, and who subsequently commanded the 68th Light Infantry. Other manuals combined light infantry service with that of conventional infantry, such as *An Exposition of the Nineteen Manoeuvres... likewise of The Exercise and Manoeuvres... for the Practice of The Light Infantry and Rifle Corps* by 'A Very Humble Patriot' (London, 1805). Such works emphasized the fact that light infantry had to be as fully conversant with ordinary infantry manoeuvres as with their specialist skills.

Training began with the officers, for, as Gross stated, 'courage alone without experience proves often insufficient against a skilful enemy. It is instruction only which can remedy this defect, and enable an officer, by applying practice to theory, to become in a short time perfect in every respect.'[21] George Napier described how this was applied in the 52nd: Col Mackenzie stated that 'the only way of having a regiment in good order was by every individual thoroughly knowing and performing his duty; and that if the officers did not fully understand their duty, it would be quite impossible to expect that the men could or would perform theirs as they ought; therefore the best and surest method was to commence drilling the

Loading on the move: a rare early depiction of the 5/60th demonstrating how light troops could load and fire without pausing – an important ability when skirmishing, and not usually practised by line troops. This rifleman is biting off the end of a cartridge.

C — THE CHAIN

'Chain order' was a method of skirmishing that differed from the ordinary skirmish line, and involved only three-quarters of a unit. At the signal to form a chain, three-quarters of the men advanced 50 paces. The remainder provided a reserve in close order (1), from which point they could either reinforce the firing-line or cover its retreat, the reserve moving as necessary to maintain the 50-pace gap.

Those who advanced (2) were divided into groups of two files (four men), each group (or 'link' in the chain) maintaining a 10-pace lateral gap between themselves and the links on either side, and the company officers (3) standing to the rear of the chain. When ordered to commence fire, the right-hand man of each link (4) advanced 3 paces and fired, then fell back to the other end of the group to reload, whereupon the second man followed suit, then the third and fourth in their turn, until the process began anew. This method permitted a more constant fire to be maintained than if the men were

operating in pairs, when there would inevitably be a pause between shots until the first man to fire had reloaded. Upon the order to retire, the chain faced-about and moved in ordinary time to close up on the reserve, which stood ready to protect them during the process.

(Inset 1) A 'link' from the 5th Bn/ 60th (Royal American) Regt, in their characteristic green jackets with red facings, c.1812. The right-hand man has just returned from firing and is priming his pan; the centre man is ramming powder and ball; and the left man is ready to step forward and fire.

(Inset 2) A pair of riflemen from the 5/60th wearing the earlier uniform of c.1800, with red-piped breeches tucked into short gaiters, depicting the standard practice of light infantrymen always operating in pairs (sometimes formally styled 'comrades'). This was essential in the skirmish-line to ensure that one of the two was always loaded and ready to protect his mate while the latter reloaded..

4

3

4

4

1

10 yds

4

2

50 yds

3

2

1

While not usual in the line, marksmanship was encouraged in the light infantry companies and regiments. Since there was no official means of recognition, medals were sometimes given at their own expense by individual officers; this silver example was presented in 1803 by Capt John Priestly of the 32nd (Cornwall) Regt to Sgt William Allen, the best shot in his light company.

whole of the officers, and when they became perfectly acquainted with the system, they could teach the men, and by their zeal, knowledge, and above all, good temper and kind treatment of the soldier, make the regiment the best in the service.'[22]

Lieutenant John Cooke of the 43rd described how officers were trained: first sent to drill with a squad of recruits to learn how to march, then how to use a musket, to shoot, and to skirmish (regimental regulations stated that officers had to be instructed by the sergeant-major). Cooke estimated that it took six months for an officer to be signed off by the adjutant as capable, and this period of serving in the ranks attuned the officer with the nature of those he was to command. Any unsuitable officers were removed without delay, and Charles Napier remarked that this made the rank-and-file say 'We had better look sharp, if he is so strict with the officers'. Periods of instruction were kept short – only an hour at a time, but four times a day – presumably so that the soldier was kept mentally fresh. Each hour's training was ended by the beat of the only drum used in the regiment, all other commands being transmitted by bugle. Twice a week the regiment paraded in full equipment so that they became used to manoeuvring under active-service conditions.

Firing practice

Although in the line infantry musketry was usually directed against compact masses, in the light infantry marksmanship was prized, and its training brought a significant tactical advantage. Its value was stressed by a number of manuals: 'To fire seldom and always with effect should be their chief study. To men who act singly or in small parties ammunition is extremely precious, and it should be husbanded with the greatest care. Noise and smoke is not sufficient to stop the advance of soldiers accustomed to war; they are to be checked only by seeing their comrades fall, and that most effectually, when they fall by the fire of an enemy who can hardly be discovered.'[23]

In a regimental order of 18 October 1803 LtCol Charles Hope of the 1st Royal Edinburgh Volunteers noted that 'the Regiment will see the folly and danger of firing at random. If their fire is ineffectual, they may as well stand to be shot at with ordered arms. Every individual must take a steady aim... let the object be to keep up a well directed fire, [rather] than a very quick fire.' Lieutenant G.B. Jackson of the 43rd noted that 'Our constant caution to the men was...*aim steadily*, and *fire low*... [The French] might fire quicker than we did, but such hurried firing scarcely admits of precision, whilst ours has been truly described as "careful and deadly."'[24]

Even though the musket was much less accurate than the rifle, light infantry undertook extensive target practice at ranges up to an astonishing 400 yards, and were taught to allow for the effect of gravity upon the ball: at 200 yards aim was taken at the middle of the enemy's body, at 300 at his headdress, and at 400 half a yard above his head.

Maintenance of fire-discipline was paramount to avoid the waste of ammunition. For example, when leading the light companies of his brigade at Bayonne, Capt William Gordon of the 50th, seeing that 'it was not without some difficulty our soldiers could be restrained from opening their fire too soon... he raised his voice to the highest pitch... when the enemy was advancing, crying out to his light companies, as they were extending to the front, "Dinna fire, men, till ye see the *wheights* of their eyes."'[25] A more basic exhortation was used by Col Robert Burns of the 36th, when a hot-headed soldier could restrain himself no longer and shot at the approaching French: Burns 'turned about, and shaking his cane, said, "Tell that Paddy O'Rafferty, if I was near him, I'd knock him down."'[26]

Skirmishing apart, firing was conducted as for the ordinary line infantry (see Osprey Elite 164, *British Napoleonic Infantry Tactics 1792–1815*). However, it was recommended that if a three-deep line were employed the front rank should load and fire as usual, while the rear rank only loaded, exchanging muskets with the middle rank, which only fired. A further drill was 'defile firing', when a unit had to engage in a confined space such as a road or gully lined with trees. A space was left at each side of the narrow frontage so that the men who had fired could withdraw to the rear to reload, successive ranks advancing to the front to fire in turn. An alternative was to leave a space down the middle through which the 'fired' men could withdraw, but Cooper's manual stated that although this looked impressive on the parade ground it was too complicated for use in action.

In addition to the designated light companies, some line battalions appear to have received some degree of light infantry training; for example, the whole of the 33rd was recorded as doing light infantry exercise in March 1814. Battalion companies could be used to augment the light infantry in action; for example, at Quatre Bras the light companies of Kempt's Brigade were reinforced by one whole company, and designated 'marksmen' from others, from the 79th. The training of such non-specialists may have been patchy, however; writing of the same action, Edward Macready of the 30th recalled that as the battalion light company was initially absent one of the others had 'endeavoured to skirmish', and had suffered heavily as a result.

Naïf but accurate depiction of techniques of firing by riflemen. On the left, a marksman shoots round the right side of the willow tree he is using for cover (prematurely, since his 'comrade' has not finished reloading). In the centre a rifleman fires prone, using his shako as a rest; at right, another fires supine, lying on his back and holding the barrel steady by bracing the sling with his foot. This last position was described in Henry Beaufoy's rifle manual *Scloppetaria* (1808) as 'not only awkward but painful', but it was occasionally used with success (as, famously, by Thomas Plunket of the 95th when he killed Gen Auguste de Colbert at Cacabellos during the retreat to Corunna).

TACTICAL DOCTRINE

Movement

Although the light infantry were fully versed in ordinary infantry tactics and manoeuvres, some aspects were peculiar to them. For movement, Dundas stated that the ordinary pace or 'step' should be 30in (76.2cm) from heel to heel, with ordinary time 75 paces to the minute, and quick time 108 paces; it was prescribed that all light infantry manoeuvres should be in quick time. There was also 'wheeling step' for changing formation, at 120 paces; 'stepping out' as a temporary measure, in which the pace was increased to 33in (83.8cm); 'stepping

(continued on page 35)

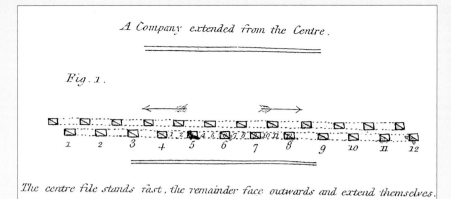

A Company extended from the Centre.

Fig. 1.

1   2   3   4   5   6   7   8   9   10   11   12

The centre file stands fast, the remainder face outwards and extend themselves.

LEFT 'Extending': diagram from an 1805 edition of the light infantry manual. The company advances from its original position (top); the central file then stands fast, while the rest of the company extends right and left from it, into a two-rank skirmish line.

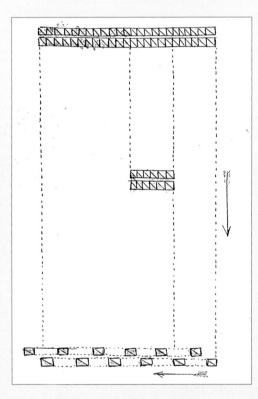
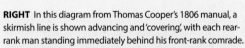

LEFT 'Extending': here the light company is shown in four sections (notionally of 12 men each). The section on the left of the line (the right, as viewed in this 1805 diagram) advances; when it reaches the required position it extends from the left into a two-rank skirmish line. The next section advances part way, to provide the support for the skirmish line; and the remaining two sections stand fast, as the reserve.

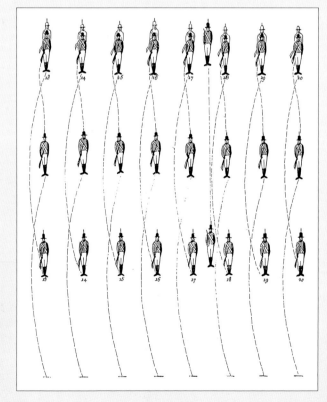

RIGHT In this diagram from Thomas Cooper's 1806 manual, a skirmish line is shown advancing and 'covering', with each rear-rank man standing immediately behind his front-rank comrade.

(Top) The front rank shields the rear rank from the enemy's fire; then the rear-rank men move around their front-rank comrades, always passing on their right side, and advance to cover them in turn. The officer (fourth man from right at top) moves straight forwards.

RIGHT 'Firing in advancing': this 1805 diagram shows (top) the rear-rank men 'stepping briskly' through the gaps in the front rank and 6 paces further, without 'covering'; they are then passed in their turn by the 'new' rear rank.

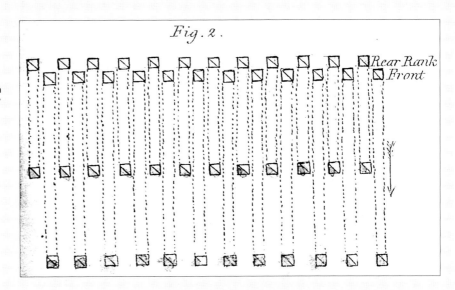

Fig. 2.

Rear Rank
Front

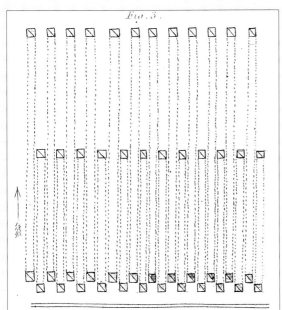

Fig. 3.

LEFT 'Firing in retreating': basically the same manoeuvre as when advancing, but here the retiring front-rank men (bottom) leave a 12-pace distance between the ranks before stopping and facing about, rather than the 6 paces left between ranks when advancing.

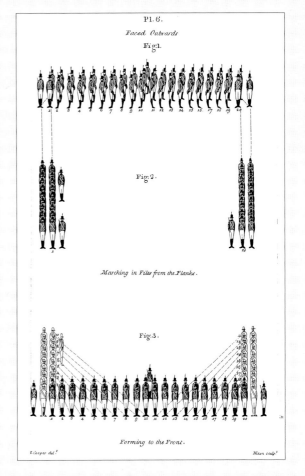

Pl. 6.
Faced Outwards
Fig. 1.

Fig. 2.

Marching in Files from the Flanks.

Fig. 3.

Forming to the Front.

T. Cooper del.   Nixon sculp.

RIGHT A company advancing in files, as shown in Thomas Cooper's 1806 manual.

(Top) From line, the two ranks face outwards from the centre; they then wheel left and right into column-of-twos, and advance to the required positions (bottom). Then they face obliquely inwards, and deploy into line once more. Note the positions of the three company officers, beside the columns rather than part of them.

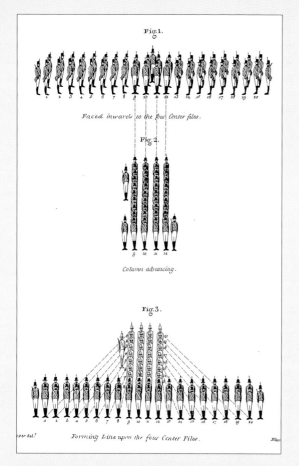

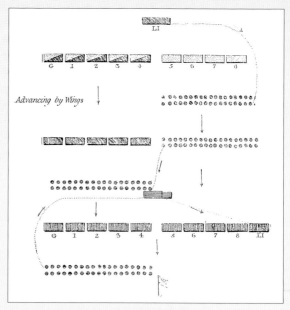

ABOVE Part of Henry Dickinson's 1798 illustration of the 16th Manoeuvre in the Dundas regulations, showing (from top to bottom) a battalion advancing by stages in two halves (wings), with the light company covering each 'lagging' wing in turn.

ABOVE A company advancing in column-of-fours, from the 1806 manual.

(Top) From line, the two ranks face inwards towards the four central files, which stand fast. The central files then advance in column-of-fours, and the remaining files feed in behind them from each side to continue the column. The whole then deploy into line once again (bottom).

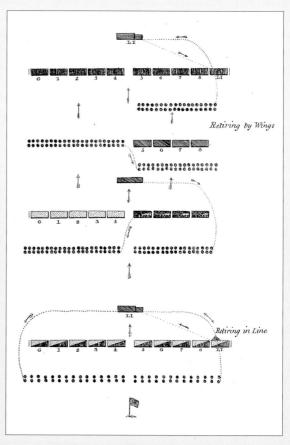

RIGHT Dickinson's 1798 diagram of Dundas's 17th Manoeuvre. (Top) A battalion retiring by wings, with the light company covering each in turn.

(Bottom) The battalion retires in line. The light company leaves its place on the left, and forms up 10 paces behind the centre of the line. It then splits into two halves, which advance around the flanks and extend in front of the line, from where they will cover the battalion's withdrawal. The manual noted that officially the light infantry were not required to form a skirmish screen on this occasion, but recommended that they did.

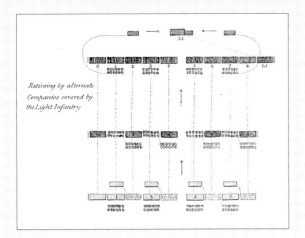

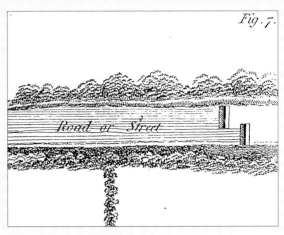

ABOVE Part of Dickinson's diagram of Dundas's 12th Manoeuvre, illustrating a battalion withdrawing by alternate individual companies. The light company has advanced in front of the line and extended into a skirmish line in four seperate sections. These then provide cover for each company as it withdraws. When all are in line in the new position (top), the light infantry sections reunite into a single body 10 paces behind the centre of the line, to await orders for the next manoeuvre.

ABOVE Defending a road – a diagram from the anonymous *A Manual for Volunteer Corps of Infantry* (1803). This shows how a road could be blocked with a barricade or abatis in two staggered halves, so that a passage was left for the defenders to sally out or retire while it still remained defensible. Thomas Cooper's *Practical Guide...* (1806) advocated lining the flanking hedgerows or walls on each side. The man at the forward end of each flanking line fired, then passed down to the other end of the line to reload. In this way a continuous fire was maintained against the head of the advancing enemy as the defenders retired slowly down each side of the road, under cover and concealing their numbers from the enemy's view.

short' to slow the rate of march without having to halt (used, for example, to permit a following unit to catch up); and marking time – marching on the spot – used similarly to avoid breaking the unit's cadence. Others included the 'side or closing step' to move a short distance to the side, and 'oblique step', to advance at an angle of about 25 degrees while still facing to the front. For light infantry, Cooper's manual mentioned 'charging time', perhaps the form of double-quick time that Neil Campbell's manual cited as 150 paces to the minute. As Cooper stated, 'executing with rapidity and vigour, is the most infallible road to victory... quickness cannot be too much inculcated in common exercise, which may prevent the bad consequences of being hurried.'

Cooper stated that troops should only run when ordered, and then only at a pace at which all could keep up and preserve order; the two men of each file were never to be separated, so the intermixing of files could be avoided. For the same reason, if a unit larger than a company were ordered to run, it was recommended that they advance in echelon with one company 6 paces behind that in front, to avoid companies becoming mixed. As shown in e.g. Plate B, such manoeuvres were often conducted in columns of two men abreast, but 'Indian files' (single file) was also sometimes employed.

For retreating there was a drill in which the right and left files stood fast to cover the withdrawal of the rest, but Cooper stated that this could cause confusion. A better system was for whole companies or sections to retire unbroken and alternately, covered by their neighbours, so that the sub-units remained intact. In such manoeuvres the ability to load and fire on the move, without pause, was important, and was a skill not usually possessed by line troops. Manningham's advice for covering an amphibious re-embarkation was surely applicable generally: 'The officers must take care that the men do not fire too fast, and that they keep sufficient quantity of ammunition, as a last resource fixing their swords [bayonets] to receive the enemy should they be inclined to charge the party retiring, and keeping up a steady fire with cartridge.'[27]

Robert Craufurd's *Standing Orders for the Light Division* included instructions for the formation and speed of march. A march was to begin in silence (with music, unless ordered otherwise) and in strict formation as if at a field day, until the order 'March at Ease' was given. Even then every man's place in the formation had to be maintained, and upon the order 'Attention' silence was reimposed and arms were sloped. To halt a column, the leading company was ordered by word of mouth, but no orders were given to those following; the succeeding companies halted automatically when they reached the prescribed distance from the one in front, and only when the last company was in position was its bugler to sound 'Halt'. (On the absence of verbal orders, Cooper noted that if one company was ordered to form in the expectation of

D **RETREATING & ADVANCING IN SECTIONS**

Further elements of skirmishing are illustrated here, featuring a notional scene in the Peninsula involving companies of Light Infantry and Rifles. In this scene the enemy are approaching from the left.

The Rifle company has deployed its skirmishers **(1)** to take advantage of natural cover in the wooded area at left, as they cover the manoeuvres of the Light Infantry. The Rifles' customary reserve **(2)**, about one-quarter of the company strength, is held back from the firing line, to reinforce it or cover its withdrawal at need.

The light infantry company **(3 & 4)**, having deployed in extended order, is now retiring to the cover of the trees at right centre as the enemy advances against them; rank **(4)** are moving, covered by rank **(3)**. Retirement was essentially the same process as advancing, but in reverse, although the distances might vary. Cooper's manual described how, on the signal to retreat, the leading rank fired, turned and marched 12 paces beyond the second rank, turned to the front, and reloaded. When the sergeant on the flank of the original second (now front) rank saw that the men behind them had finished reloading he blew his whistle; thereupon the now-front rank fired, faced about, and marched to the rear of the now-second rank, and the leap-frogging process began again. 'Thus, alternately, each rank retires, supporting each other. At the signal to halt, they cease firing, and the rear rank instantly closes.' **(5)** indicates the position of an officer, just behind the firing line; the other two would be positioned similarly, with the company commander in the centre (here out of the picture to the right).

Another company advances in support **(6)** from its starting position in line **(7)**, by four columns of two men abreast, running forward to their intended destination on the bank of the stream, where they will extend in line. The company's three officers advance level with the heads of three of the columns-of-twos.

A sergeant of the light company of 1/Coldstream Guards recalled back-and-forth skirmishing actions against French *voltigeurs* in olive groves at Talavera on 29 June 1809. The French 'opened a most galling fire from the shelter of the Olive trees, this threw our Brigade into disorder & we retired rather in an irregular manner, however having regained the ground, we advanced, firm, our Brigade reformed, & poured

in a couple of well directed vollies, which did great execution & they retired in turn persued [sic] by the light Companies. At this time having obtained entrance in the Olive Grove occupied by them the Skirmishers on both sides singled out their objects, & thus for 10 or 15 minutes were amusing ourselves shooting at one another as deliberately as if we had been Pigeon Shooting... The object I had singled out, & myself exchanged three rounds each, the second of his, hit me slightly on the right Shoulder, & after my third he disappeared therefore I conclude he went home! In this service all advantages are taken to conceal One's self if possible, therefore where a tree or other object presents itself it is made use of as a Shelter.'

Shortly after this the French rallied and drove the skirmishers out of the wood, but the sergeant and two men of his company failed to hear the bugles sound the recall. By the time they realized they were alone the enemy were within 20 or 30 yards: 'therefore nothing but flight could prevent us falling into their hands, & facing about away we started & were instantly saluted with a Shower of Musketry & which was continued until we reached our Line, nothing less than a miracle could have saved us, balls were loged [sic] in our clothes & knapsacks, yet unhurt!'. (Anonymous MS in author's possession.)

(Inset) The Brunswick Oels Corps was one of the foreign units used to supplement the regular light infantry. The exiled Duke of Brunswick took his black-clad 'legion', originally in Austrian pay, into British service after Napoleon's defeat of Austria in 1809. The Brunswick Oels Jägers were sent to the Peninsula in 1810, originally 12 companies strong; three were subsequently detached and deployed as individual skirmisher companies like those of the 5/60th Rifles. The main body served in the 4th, 7th, and Light Divisions, the separate companies in the 4th and 5th Divisions and attached to the 1st Division at the passage of the Bidassoa. Some – perhaps the detached companies – wore green jackets with light blue facings, but the unit's principal uniform was black, with the death's-head shako badge that gave rise to the nickname 'death-or-glory men'. Though effective skirmishers, the unit's original Brunswickers became diluted with various German-speaking odds-and-ends, and it had a poor record for desertion; Craufurd remarked that if any wished to go over to the enemy, he would gladly issue them with a pass to that effect.

action, all the others were to follow suit even if they had received no order to that effect.) 'Stepping out' to catch up the company in front was forbidden; if a gap opened the leading company was to 'step short' until the follower had caught up, thus preventing hurry and breaks in formation. Unless unavoidable, 'defiling' or deviation from the line of march to avoid an obstacle was forbidden; Craufurd (like Wellington himself) was known to berate officers who attempted to keep their feet dry when crossing water.

Craufurd was equally unforgiving of straggling. A man unable to continue from fatigue could only fall out once he had a ticket from his company commander; those without tickets were court-martialled immediately and punished (usually flogged) when they caught up, and only complete physical collapse was an acceptable excuse for not requesting a ticket. Any who fell out for a call of nature had to leave their musket and knapsack with their comrades as an incentive for re-joining immediately. (Gross advocated that those who fell out for such a purpose should be made to hurry ahead of the column first so as not to lag behind, and when they had finished should wait for the unit to catch them up before re-joining.)

Although not published until 1814, Craufurd's regulations for the Light Division were in operation from 1809, and in addition to aiding order and discipline they may also have helped to inculcate the higher morale expected of light infantry.

The legacy of Shorncliffe

The techniques of light infantry tactics were specified in the manuals, but at least as significant was the practical application that came initially from intensive training. Arguably the most celebrated training camp that ever existed was that superintended by Moore at Shorncliffe, outside Folkestone in Kent, where the three regiments that were to form the Light Division in the Peninsula received their schooling: the 43rd, 52nd, and 95th. Captain John Paul Hopkins of the 43rd, who served from the Talavera campaign to the Pyrenees, summarized the legacy of Shorncliffe:

'There officers were formed for command, and soldiers acquired such discipline as to become an example to the army and proud of their profession... though drill was an important part of the instruction, it was not... by that alone the soldier was there formed. It was the internal and moral system, the constant superintendence of the officers, which carried the discipline to such perfection... by their discipline they sustained [their] character throughout the war, committing no blunders, and showing themselves the same orderly soldiers on the breach as in the line.'[28]

In addition to what was specified in the regulations, it is likely that practices evolved on campaign, and such amendments were not exclusive to the Peninsula. For example, referring to the Foot Guards' flank battalions in the Netherlands in April 1794, an officer of the Coldstream noted: 'Out for two hours this Morn'g march'ng in Line & form'g open Columns – In consequence of an order from Prince Coburg the Rear Rank of each Batt'n is to form a reserve – 2 deep – 50 paces in the Rear of the Batt'n to support the Right or Left Flanks as may be most essential.'[29]

Skirmishing: theory, and practice

The cornerstone of light infantry tactics was skirmishing, as depicted in Plates A–D. The two principal formations were 'extended' and 'open order', both employing two ranks. Although extended order varied according to

Light infantry on campaign, *c*.1800, following the introduction of the 'stovepipe' shako (centre) but without the large plate worn by battalion and grenadier companies. The other figures wear undress fatigue caps of 'tea-cosy' shape, or possibly old-fashioned light infantry caps. The standing man still has the old lapelled coat cut away over the stomach, which was officially replaced from 1797. (Engraving by and after W.M. Pyne, 1802)

circumstances and terrain, officially the ranks were 6 paces apart with 2 paces between the files; officers were positioned behind the rear rank, the company commander in the centre and the subalterns towards each flank. The sergeants were posted to the rear of each rank, although some manuals suggest they were sometimes level with the men. In open order the files were only 2ft (61cm) apart, with the officers 3 paces in front of the line, the company commander at the right in line with the second file from the flank, the second-in-command similarly on the left, and the most junior officer in the centre.

Skirmish lines were formed by 'extending', which could be done from the centre, left, or right. The men would move from column in quick time and with weapons at the trail, facing right or left and moving in that direction until they reached the required point, when they faced towards the enemy. If the lateral gaps between files were required to be more than 2 paces, the officers would call out the distance. Neil Campbell stated that 12-pace gaps were common, and that the men should use their initiative to halt where cover was best available, and not attempt to dress the line – 'a waving rough line of skirmishers is equally good', providing that decent cover could be found. It was recommended that when the required spot was reached the men should kneel; and that when 'close' was ordered the process should be reversed, but with the men at shoulder-arms.

Although it was advocated that when a line was formed the flanks should be thrown back as a form of protection, a writer in the *United Service Journal* in 1829 claimed that far from protecting the flanks, this permitted the enemy to fire into the flanks of the central body before the flank-guards could come up; it had been Moore's practice at Shorncliffe that the main body and flanks were in line. He also criticized the practice by which the flanking parties moved diagonally before extending inwards from the flanks. This, he stated, took longer and was more difficult than advancing directly forwards and extending from the centre to the flanks. Such statements suggest that variations on the standard drill did indeed evolve at regimental level.

Rottenburg included instructions for advancing by platoons or sections, in which one sub-unit would advance 60 yards and extend to cover the frontage before the neighbouring sub-unit could follow – in effect advancing by 'bounds', so that advancing units would always be covered by their neighbours.

Cooper stated that 'It is a first principle in the war of Light Troops, that a considerable portion of their force should at all times be kept in reserve'. Usually there would be two reserves: one immediately behind the skirmish line, and another further back to act as a rallying-point in case of retreat. Cooper advocated that no more than half a unit should be sent forward to skirmish until a second whole unit could act as the reserve. The regulation stated that the first reserve should be 13 paces behind the skirmish line, but Cooper said that this was rarely applied; such a gap was insufficient to permit manoeuvre, and was used mainly for reviews. It was recommended that when the first reserve was sent forward to reinforce the skirmish line, it should extend into skirmish order before reaching the front, and then advance into and through the gaps in the initial line.

E SCOUTING

This plate illustrates aspects of the vital duty of reconnaissance, as performed by the light company of a line battalion or one of the companies of a light battalion. Cooper's manual stated that 'No body of troops ought at any time to march without an advanced guard; and a communication should be constantly kept up between the advanced guard and the main body.' This illustrates the process by which that could be accomplished.

The main body of nine companies is advancing in column (1), with mounted officers on one flank and at the rear. The light company was sent forward some 500 paces (only 300 at night, or in hazy weather); the company commander and a section – one-quarter of the company – remained there as a reserve (2) to the reconnaissance parties. A further section (or quarter) of the company was advanced a further 200 paces (3), from which point a sergeant and six men were pushed on a further 100 paces (4) to form the very head of the advanced guard. The two remaining sections were sent out 300 paces laterally from the reserve to cover the flanks (5), and from each of these a sergeant and six men (6) were thrown out another 100 paces in an oblique direction. From these small parties, individual scouts were sent out even further forward and on the flanks of the detached party (7). When moving, the various advanced parties would move at the same speed as the main body to preserve the distances, and would thus represent something akin to fingers stretching out from hands, themselves extended away from the body.

These duties, notably those of the most advanced sentries, emphasized the importance of initiative and intelligence on the part of private soldiers who were operating some distance from their NCOs. When ordered to concentrate, upon the first signal to 'close' the individual scouts and sergeants' parties would run back to join their sections; and upon the second signal to 'close' the three advanced sections would fall back to join the reserve.

When posted as sentries to screen a static position rather than scouts for a moving body, the men usually operated in pairs so that one could carry a message back to the nearest supporting post. George Gleig of the 85th mentioned another advantage of sending out pairs: that if he was posted on a recent battlefield the presence of the dead might so un-nerve a solitary man that he might be impelled to leave his post. He recalled how one such sentry was found having fainted, and, at the risk of his comrades' ridicule, claimed that a white figure had crawled towards him, moaning, and as he was about to issue a challenge a dead man beside him sat up!

A typical instance of night scouting was recalled by the light-company sergeant of 1/Coldstream, on the night of 29/30 June 1809 at Talavera: 'Towards dusk... the Enemy made a show of maneurveing [sic] with Cavalry in our front... In order to ascertain... their indication of movement myself & my file coverer were detached to the front under cover of the dark by [Col the Hon Edward Stopford, 3rd Guards] to within half a Pistol shot of them with orders to return in as quick as possible should they remove to their front; however this was nothing more than a feint to cover the retreat of their Artillery & Infantry & the whole had disappeared by daybreak.'

(Inset) At night the approach of an enemy might be signalled by a shot, or the carrying of the news by one of the pair of sentries. When visual signals could be seen, however, it was recommended that one sentry should hold up his shako on the end of his musket to signal the approach of a small party, or that both men should do so to notify an advance in force. Cooper noted that sentries on duty were not permitted to 'support' or 'slope' their musket, but should hold it at the ready, supported on the left arm, as favoured by riflemen.

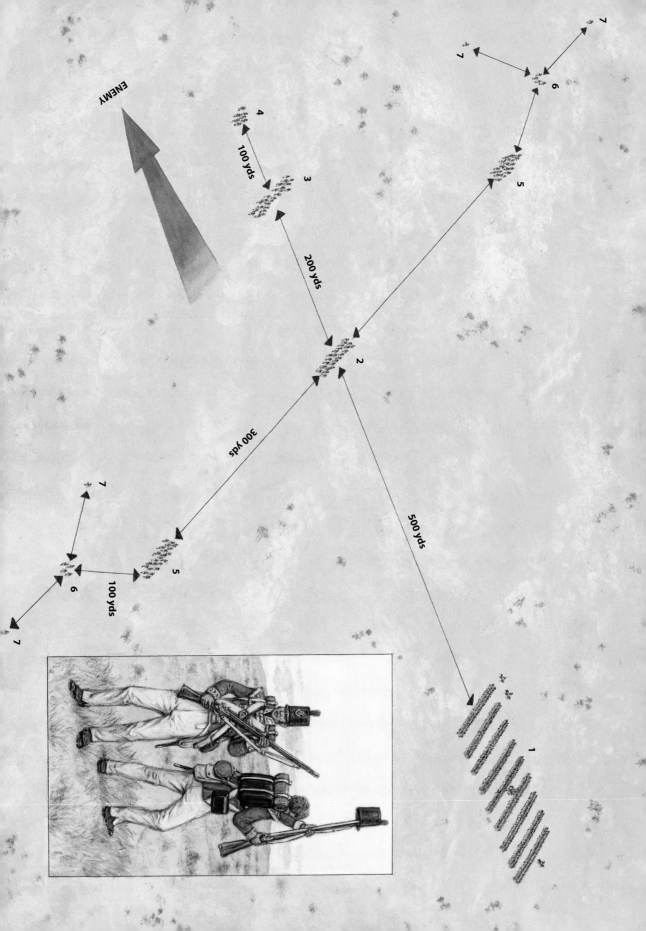

ENEMY

4

100 yds

3

200 yds

5

6

7

7

7

300 yds

2

500 yds

5

100 yds

6

7

7

1

Another article in the *United Service Journal* in 1829 described a variation claimed to have been employed with success. Four companies formed the skirmish line, with a supporting company in column behind each flank, and the battalion's remaining four companies in reserve further back, in quarter-distance columns. If the supporting companies behind the flanks had to reinforce the skirmish line, two of the reserve companies would take their place, but two companies would always remain in the rear to form a rallying-point. Sergeants were always detached from the forward companies and remained with the reserve, so that men having to retreat from the front would recognize them and be able to re-form on their own sergeants.

In the skirmish line, Cooper described the mode of firing: 'It is to be a standing rule, that the two men of the same file are never unloaded together; for which purpose, as soon as the front rank man has fired, he is to slip round the left of the rear rank man, who will make a short pace forward, and put himself in the other's place, whom he is to protect while loading. When the first man returns his ramrod, he will give his comrade the word *ready*, after which, and not before, he may fire, and immediately change place as before.'

When advancing, on the order to commence fire, the rear rank moved 6 paces in front of the front rank and fired; whereupon the sergeant of the front rank whistled to signal the original front rank to advance 6 paces in front of those who had just fired, and themselves fired once the original firers had reloaded. This process operated in reverse when retreating, when Cooper stated: 'The skirmishers must keep up a good countenance, and avoid hurry. They must endeavour to gall the enemy from every favourable situation, and make him pay dearly for the ground he acquires. The reserves, if not pressed upon by the skirmishers, will be able to give them... effectual support.' Gross stated that when defending a position the skirmish line should remain static except for the front and rear ranks continually changing places to fire, with the reserve only used in the event of an enemy breakthrough.

When approaching a contested bridge, the practice was for the skirmish line to close up to the centre at a run, cross the bridge in column, and extend again left and right, with the reserve following. The *United Service Journal* commentator described a preferred tactic: the skirmish line was to line the riverbank, while the reserve crossed the bridge in column covered by the fire of the bank-liners. The reserve would then extend into a skirmish line themselves, and the bank-liners closed up, crossed the bridge in column, and then acted as the reserve for the new skirmish line.

If threatened by cavalry, the usual protection of forming square was often impossible for a skirmish line, so alternatives were described. The light troops could stand firm and fire from cover, or form small rallying squares or 'orbs' (Cooper used the term 'round mass'), and once the cavalry had veered away they should retire to the nearest cover, not even pausing to re-load. Gross advocated that the skirmishers should close and form in two ranks with a 'crochet' on each flank (presumably a 'refused' flank thrown back), and the front rank kneeling. When the cavalry came within 25 yards the rear rank should fire, then the front rank stand and fire, the whole then presenting their bayonets, with a third rank, if one existed, reserving its fire for emergencies. The 1829 commentator stated that there were occasions in the Peninsula when light infantry stood their ground in this way; on such occasions any supporting detachment should advance to reinforce the skirmish line rather than the latter falling back on the support, as such a retreat might demoralize the men and lead to disorder.

The Coldstream at Talavera

In a manuscript in the author's possession, an anonymous sergeant of the light company of the 1st Bn Coldstream Guards describes aspects of the tactics and hazards of the skirmish line at Talavera on 27–28 July 1809. The first episode echoes the tactics illustrated in Plate G, and the second the inherent danger of deployment in front of the main infantry line. (The original spelling is preserved, but the officers mentioned are identified in added parentheses):

'The firing of small Arms did not begin untill dusk when the Enemy foolishly attempted to impose upon [us. They] were suffered to advance nearly to the summit when the light infantry of Genl Hill's division opened a fire upon them & retreated, by this they were deceived, & pressed further on & the Line then poured several vollies into them charged & bayonnetted them back again.

'Shortly after this a dreadful mistake occurred which involved the safety of no less than the lives of the whole of the light Infantry who had formed a chain of communication from one flank to the other in front of the Line. By a sudden impulse on the left [of the main line] the ranks commenced a kind of firing resembling a feu de joye, which communicated from one Battalion to the other & ran down with the rapidity of lightening, & by this our Battalion alone had one Lieut Col [John Ross] mortally wounded & our Adjutant [Lt & Capt George Bryan] was also wounded in three places & expired in the hands of the French... Our company had also one man very severely wounded & was afterwards made prisoner. The 3d Regiment had one man killed on the spot. The left sections of the Lt Infantry were not more than 25 yards from the muzzles of the firelocks & I who was one of them seeing what was likely to happen ordered the whole of my section to lay down on their faces & thus probably preserved my life for that time.' (It was recorded elsewhere that John Ross fell at the head of the battalion's grenadiers, so perhaps that company was here used in the older way, joined with the light infantry in the skirmish line.)

Although some of the uniform details are wrong for the stated identity of this unit (the 85th Light Infantry, at the Nivelle), and would be more appropriate for the light company of a line battalion, this later illustration nevertheless accurately reflects a skirmish line in action. The men are in open order, operating in pairs or advancing at the trail, and the officer is accompanied by his bugler. (Print after Richard Simkin)

Reconnaissance

When Coote Manningham delivered his lectures to his officers at Shorncliffe in 1803, the entire content of all four concerned reconnaissance, scouting, and patrolling, and the situations that might be encountered. A considerable proportion was derived directly from Gross's manual. Manningham summarized this service thus:

'Light troops are, as it were, a light or beacon for the General, which should constantly inform him of the situation, the movements, and nature of the enemy's designs; it is upon the exactness and intelligence of what they report that he is enabled to regulate the time and manner of executing his own enterprises... The safety of an army, the justness of those measures which have so direct an influence upon success, depend frequently upon the vigilance, the expertness, and the superiority of the light troops compared with those of the enemy.'

Gross advocated a mixed force of infantry and light cavalry. The infantry were to scout at night, and in daylight to operate on the flanks of the cavalry, with skirmishers in front and a reserve at the rear; at night the infantry should be gathered on only one flank, so as not to risk shooting each other in the dark. As usual, he argued that the retention of a reserve was essential, to check any enemy pursuit of those in front.

In reconnoitring a village, Gross stated that the outskirts should be scouted, and that a couple of 'the most respectable inhabitants' should be questioned; the scouts 'should treat them civilly, but at the same time declare to them, that if the enemy should be concealed in the houses of the village without their giving information of it, they will be shot instantly.' Any information from enemy deserters should be treated with suspicion, for 'having been once a rogue [by deserting] he will most probably continue so.'

Outpost duty

One of the light infantry's most important services was the 'outpost'– the provision of a screen of sentries between the enemy and the army they were tasked with protecting, to prevent incursions and deny the enemy's scouts the opportunity to gather intelligence. The Light Division excelled in this duty in the Peninsula; it was claimed that they were never surprised and that their line of outposts was never penetrated, ensuring the security of the army at all times. The essentials of the technique resembled that illustrated on Plate E.

Coote Manningham stated that in the proximity of the enemy sentries should be posted in pairs, so that one could carry news to the immediate supporting post; 150 paces to the rear, this should typically consist of an NCO and a party of four or six other ranks. Behind them was the main supporting party, which would have established a defensive position against any enemy incursion; bridges could be blocked or have their planks removed, and Manningham recommended the fortification of a building such as a church to act as a redoubt. Gross recommended using walls or hedges as the basis of defence, as buildings could be set alight, and he believed that light infantry should always have maximum freedom of movement and not be confined within buildings. (This is only one of a number of his tactical principles which the modern equivalents of the old light infantry would certainly endorse.)

Manningham advised that the advanced sentry posts be relieved every one or two hours, with patrols sent out at least hourly in front of the sentry-line to investigate any movement or noise from the enemy side. On hearing someone approach, the sentry should advance and shout 'Halt, who comes there?', and should fire if there were no reply or if an incorrect countersign (password) were given. At night there should be regular inspection of sentries to ensure that they were awake, and they were never to smoke, 'neither read, whistle, or sing, or even speak to any one unless it be necessary', but always to listen intently, to which end they should never put up their hood if their greatcoat had one. While patrolling, 'however bad the weather [they] must not be suffered to put on their watch coats'. Gross added that sentries might smoke in daylight, but always with a cover on their pipe (note that Gross came from a Germanic background, where pipes with covers were quite traditional; British soldiers smoked short clays, lacking such refinements).

On the approach of an enemy, Manningham stated that a shot should be fired to give the alarm, and that any enemy coming to parley should be made to face the way he had come, so as not to see the post's defences. (Conversely, Gross advised not firing a shot as a signal in case it led to confusion, but instead recommended 'some other method, as whistling or hallooing'). Manningham stated that if a post were driven in, the sentries should not retire directly upon their supports but make a detour to avoid leading the enemy onto them. If a main post were overrun the men should disperse and make their way individually to a predetermined rallying-point, to ensure that at least one man got back to carry news of the enemy's advance.

Gross noted that a patrol might need to attack an enemy outpost. In such a case he advocated the use of a vanguard and two reserves, the first to support the vanguard and attack any enemy reinforcements, and the second to pursue a beaten enemy or act as a rallying point if the first two parties had to retire. For attacking at night he advised that the party be divided in two, with a rope 50 or 60 yards long stretched between them. By pulling on it once, a signal could be given to retire, and two pulls could be the signal for both parties to attack from their separate locations, and 'this scheme may also be practised to lay an ambuscade of riflemen any where.'

Outpost duty required the initiative and self-reliance that was a feature of light infantry, as sentries were usually without the supervision of a senior rank. William Napier recounted a notable incident involving two privates of his company of the 43rd who were watching the crossing of the river Esla at Castro Gonzalo on the night of 26 December 1808. An attack by French cavalry who aimed to surprise them resulted in a remarkable display of courage: 'John Walton and Richard Jackson, private soldiers of the forty-third, being posted beyond the bridge, were directed, on the approach of an enemy, the one to stand fast, the other to fire and run back to the brow of the hill, to give notice whether there were many or few. Jackson fired, but was overtaken, and received twelve or fourteen cuts in an instant; nevertheless he came staggering on, and gave the signal, while Walton, with equal resolution, stood his ground, and wounded several of his assailants, who then retired, leaving him unhurt, but his cap, knapsack, belts, and musket, were cut in above twenty places, and his bayonet bent double, and notched like a saw.'[30] Jackson recovered from his injuries.

A notable feature of the Peninsular War was the 'live-and-let-live' system maintained between the British and French outposts, as described by Charles Parker Ellis of the 1st Foot Guards: 'I never knew an advanced sentry of either army to be *wantonly* shot at the out-posts; and I have often myself, when strolling too far in advance of my own piquet [sic], been saved

Silhouette of Maj Richard Hungerford Elers, who led the 43rd at Fuentes de Oñoro. When he died four months later on 29 August 1811, of a fever 'brought on by his unremitting exertions', the regiment to which he had been 'so sincere a friend' wore mourning for three days. Note the bugle-horn device on the shako and above the '43' on the bi-metal belt-plate, and the conventional epaulettes rather than wings.

The characteristic appearance of light infantry in 1814, though depicted here for a home-defence unit – the East York Militia. The shoulder wings are smaller and more practical for light infantry service than those of the grenadier in the right background. (Engraving by George Walker)

by the French, but in no one instance was I fired upon.'[31]

Frederick Mainwaring of the 51st concurred: 'This is the real chivalry of modern warfare, and robs it of half its horrors... the French and English soldier had no feeling of animosity towards each other; they fought bravely in the field, but on piquets [sic] they have been known for days to be within musket-shot, but sentinels perhaps separated only by a ditch, yet not a shot was ever fired except at the proper time. They knew how useless it was to harass each other for nothing, and though they both did their duty in the most vigilant manner, confidence was never abused, and we frequently conversed familiarly with the French officers at the advanced posts with as much feeling of security as in our own tents.'[32]

Charles Parker Ellis recalled a not untypical incident on a picquet line in the Peninsula: 'Our sentry... called us up to him and pointed out a French sentry who had just been posted immediately on the other side of the hedge, and quite within our lines. Col Alexander... told him that he must go off. The man replied, that he dare not leave his post, but that when the relief came, he would tell "Monsieur le Caporal" what the Colonel said. Alexander desired him to beckon up some one... [and when an officer came up Alexander told him] that he had no wish to hurt the sentry, but that if he was not withdrawn in a quarter of an hour he would be shot. The French officer was a very reasonable and gentleman-like young man; and after many bows, and the exchange of a pinch of snuff, he went back to his party, taking the sentry with him.'[33]

This relaxed attitude extended to the other ranks, as in an encounter recalled by George Landmann of the 50th, when opposing picquets, separated only by a ditch, attempted to chat. The Frenchman threw the Englishman a large piece of bread; 'John Bull could not be out-done in liberality by mounseer, so down he stepped into the ditch, holding up his canteen', and inviting the Frenchman to 'take a drop to old Georgey's health'. This was accepted with demonstrative gratitude; however, the English sentry violently misinterpreted the Frenchman's embrace and kisses, and Landmann had to step in to restore the peace.[34]

LIGHT INFANTRY ON CAMPAIGN

The value of experience
The need for effective light troops was brought into especial focus in the Peninsula due to the excellence of the French light infantry, as observed by John Patterson of the 50th:

Death in no-man's-land

One of the grislier dangers of fighting over the ground between the main lines of battle is recalled in the anonymous account of Talavera left by the light infantry sergeant of 1/Coldstream, quoted above:

'Shot & shells were not the only danger presented to the contending armies for the intermediate space of ground between the lines was covered partly with standing corn & high stubble which from the incessant firing kept up by both sides, was set ablaze several times during the day, & Lines of running fire half a mile in length were frequent & fatal to many a Soldier, some by their pouches blowing up in passing the fire, others Wounded unable to reach their respective Armies lying weltering in their gore with the devouring element approaching & a death most horrid staring them in the face! Thus perished many & amongst the rest our Major of Brigade [Lt & Capt Richard Beckett] one of the most gallant & at the same time useful Officers in his Majesty's service when in the act of rallying the Brigade after retiring in disorder, he was knocked off his horse & fell a victim to the flames before assistance could be given.'

'On a surface as flat as a billiard-table, the Frenchman hides himself, merely stretching along the earth, like some deadly reptile, taking his cap as a rest for his fusil. Or he will creep within a few yards of the object he would aim at, and seldom misses. The slightest possible elevation is sufficient for him. Our fellows are not so ingenious in this way... the red jackets in particular must have cover.'[35]

Patterson emphasized the importance of experience as well as training, citing an instance at the battle of Vimeiro when some battalion companies had to support the light troops:

'Getting bewildered among the corn-fields and olives, the young hands scarcely knew which way to turn, the old ones, too, were puzzled, and when a blaze of musketry opened on them, from they knew not where, after firing at random a few shots in the air, they were literally mowed down, falling like ninepins amid the standing corn... The writer of these pages was on that duty, the emergency of which was so deeply impressed upon his mind, that he has never since forgotten it... Capt [Arthur] Coote, of the 50th... seeing the havoc among his helpless soldiers, sent an officer for a section of the Rifles; but before aid should come... he was shot through the heart by a musket-ball.' Patterson then remarked upon a newly-arrived light battalion:

'A finer, more robust, and healthy-looking body of soldiers it would be difficult to find, but, poor fellows: "the pipe-clay was soon shook out of their jackets", for getting somehow exposed to a galling range of fire, they were most severely handled, whole sections of them lying, as they fell, in the dykes and hollows where they had been stationed. With scarcely anything beyond a smattering of Dundass [sic], with sundry evolutions at the double-quick, their military education was supposed to be complete, but the men knew nothing of the business of a rifleman.'[36] (One should note that Patterson's comments on this battalion – the 43rd – were refuted by one of its members.) Patterson claimed that 'The 95th... with a battalion of the 60th, were the only light troops that could be effectually brought into play as Rifles... reduced to skeletons over and over again, [their ranks] were as often filled, for they were thrown in the face of every danger, nor could any enterprise be undertaken without their aid.'[37]

Despite the notably stoic tone of many of the few memoirs we have from the ranks, it should not be supposed that the men who endured such relentless service never suffered psychologically. Frederick Mainwaring of the 51st recalled an occasion when, in full expectation of a French advance, the reserve to a picquet line had been permitted to 'lie down in the village church, with loaded arms in our hands. In the middle of the night, when all were sound asleep, worn out with fatigue and anxiety, suddenly the most piercing shrieks broke upon the stillness of the church. In an instant the men were on their legs, and, conceiving that the enemy were upon them, they began a most tremendous fire. Some rushed to the door – others were thrown down and trampled upon – and never did I experience such a sensation of horror, as, waking suddenly out of a sound sleep, these horrid yells rung in my ears. All this lasted but a few seconds; and when order was restored it appeared that the innocent cause of all this uproar and confusion was one of the soldiers, who... dreaming that some one was cutting his throat, screamed out in this terrific manner... and fired his musket.'[38]

Despite the wear-and-tear on the veterans, however, the greater vulnerability of newly arrived soldiers was noted as late as 1815. Edward Costello of the 95th stated that 'It is remarkable to see recruits in action generally more unfortunate than experienced soldiers; this I have often noticed. We had many fine recruits, who had only joined us on the eve of our leaving England, killed here. The reason of this is, that an old soldier will seek shelter from the enemy's fire if [there is] any near his post, while the inexperienced recruit appears, as it were, petrified to the spot by the whizzing balls.'[39]

LIGHT COMPANY COVERING DEPLOYMENT OF BATTALION

A battalion could be vulnerable during deployment from column into line, and its light company played a crucial role in shielding it from the enemy until its new position was established. This depicts a line battalion moving from column to line, deploying from the right.

The right-flank company stood firm; the others faced left, marched parallel to the intended position in line, then faced right and advanced successively into their places in the line. During this manoeuvre, the light company advanced (green arrows) to cover the battalion's frontage from their position in column – usually in twos, with a half-company on each flank of the battalion. Upon the order to deploy, the light company doubled to a position ahead of the intended battalion line, half of them advancing to the front and the other half obliquely to a position mid-way along the intended front. Both halves then 'extended' into a skirmish line in the usual way, thus shielding the deploying battalion from enemy sight and providing a buffer against enemy skirmishers. When the line was formed the light company could fall back in two halves, closing up to the flanks and retiring to a position on or to the rear of each flank.

(Inset 1) An important facet in the system of command-and-control was the light infantry bugle. Buglers were used by light regiments in place of the drummers of the line regiments, but it was stated that bugle-calls should be used to augment, rather than replace, verbal commands, especially over distances. (Cooper's manual stated that 'A good bugle may be heard at the distance of three miles.') As early as 1774 the Inspection Return of the 3rd Foot (Buffs) noted that a trumpet was used to call back the light company; presumably when it was first deploying the officers' verbal commands could be heard.

Cooper wrote that as soon as a bugle was heard the troops should 'mark time', presumably until the call could be understood. A low 'G' was sounded first as a caution before the actual call; then two 'Gs' if a movement were to be made from the right, one if from the centre, and three if from the left. Calls were initially unregulated, but a work on bugle sounds appeared in 1795. In 1799 a version of the manual ordered by the Duke of York the previous year by James Hyde, trumpet-major of the London and Westminster Light Horse Volunteers, included light infantry calls as used by the Foot Guards. Cooper's manual listed 37 calls for the field and 14 for use in barracks, but stated that those actually used should be 'few and simple' and well understood by officers and NCOs. According to Cooper, only five were essential: Advance, Retreat, Halt, Cease Fire, and Assemble. The illustration shows a light company officer of the 2nd (Coldstream) Guards in the uniform of 1812–15, with his bugler in close attendance, distinguished by the blue-and-white musicians' lace on his jacket.

(Inset 2) Typical uniform for light infantry at the turn of the 18th/19th centuries. This depicts a soldier and an officer of the 90th (Perthshire Volunteers), the first regular regiment during the period to be trained as light infantry. The original uniform of the rank-and-file included grey pantaloons (hence the regimental nickname 'Perthshire Greybreeks'), worn with short light-infantry gaiters, and a Tarleton helmet which carried a bugle-horn badge above the peak. In the Egyptian campaign of 1801 the regiment was commanded by Rowland Hill, later Wellington's most trusted deputy, and at Alexandria it formed the advance guard with the 92nd Highlanders. It was said that the Tarleton helmets caused the French to mistake them for dismounted cavalry and thus easy prey; but when the 2e Chasseurs à Cheval charged impetuously while the 90th was changing formation the Perthshire shattered them with musketry without forming square. One wing closed up to form a column six or eight deep, and held off a renewed French attack until the army caught up..

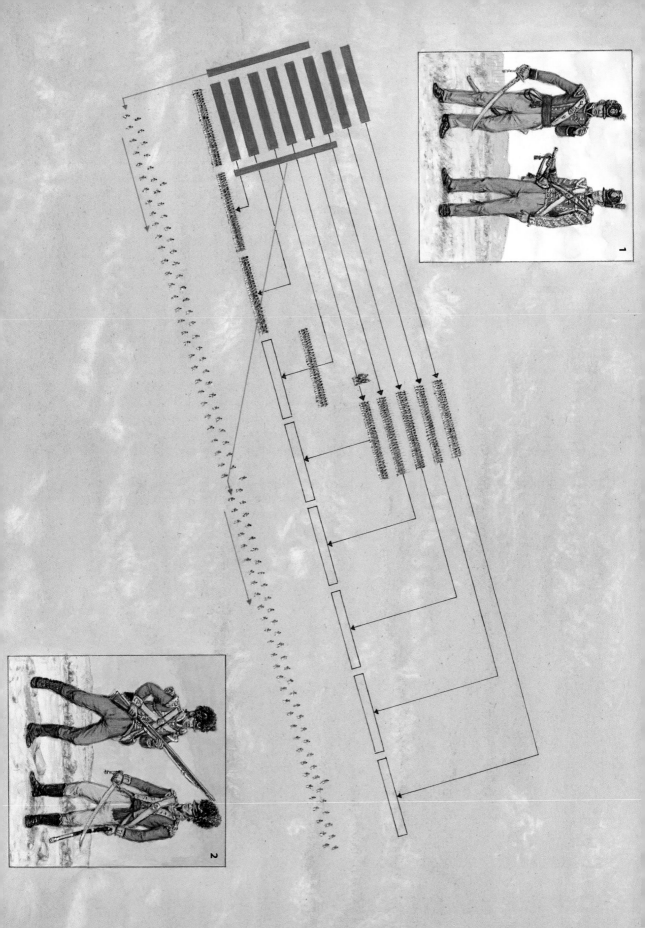

Foreign corps

The quality of the German emigré corps is exemplified by a recollection from Walcheren by Capt John Ford, 79th Highlanders, presumably referring to sharpshooters of one of the light battalions of the King's German Legion:

'A French officer sent to reconnoitre our posts, raised his head in a field of corn, and most unexpectedly found himself close to a picquet of German riflemen in our service. A salute from the Germans made him drop down for concealment in the corn, and crawling along on all fours for some distance, he would rise again in another part and run a little in an erect position, when pop, pop, pop, from the Germans obliged him to drop again, he was up and down in this way till he made his escape. The Germans were laughing all the time, and as they knew not in what part of the corn he would rise to run a little, they did not take aim till his cocked hat made its appearance.'[40] Perhaps the riflemen were deriving so much amusement from the Frenchman's discomfiture that they were deliberately aiming to scare, rather than hit him.

Light-company man of a line battalion: a self-portrait by William Payne of the 1st Foot Guards in the uniform of 1812–15. It shows a green plume and shako cords, and a distinctive light company shako badge of a bugle-horn above a star device. Payne served in the Peninsula and at Walcheren. (Courtesy Dr John A. Hall)

To increase the numbers of light infantry in the Peninsular army the old expedient of using foreign troops was notably effective in the case of the Portuguese Caçadores. These units were trained in the British system; their manual, *Systema de Instrucção e Discipline para os Movimentos e Deveres dos Caçadores*, was Neil Campbell's work translated by William Warre, sometime ADC to Marshal Beresford. Warre commented in a letter to his father in December 1809 that it was 'a tiresome undertaking, but most necessary, and for the appearance of which I am much hurried.' Previously he had translated Dundas's infantry manual, which had 'already been of essential use, and gained me some credit.'[41] He finished the light infantry manual in February 1810, and it was published in Lisbon later that year.

To complete the integration of the Caçadores into the British system, British officers were appointed at field and company level. About one-third were transferred from British light infantry or rifle corps, so had experience of light infantry service. They included, for example, Sgt Johann Schwalback of the 60th, commissioned captain in the 6th Caçadores; one from the York Light Infantry Volunteers, and two from the Royal West India Rangers. Lieutenant-Colonel Kenneth Snodgrass, who commanded the 1st Caçadores in the later stages of the war, had wide experience of service in the 90th, 43rd, and (at Moore's behest) the 52nd, so was ideally suited to lead a light battalion.

Another addition to the army's light infantry was the Brunswick Oels Corps (see inset, Plate D), which served as a battalion and also – like the 5/60th – had rifle companies posted individually to augment the existing divisional light troops. The 'Brunswick Owls' were as expert riflemen as the 60th, and by providing rifle-armed sharpshooters throughout the army augmented one of its most important resources.

LEFT A copy of the Portuguese translation of Col Neil Campbell's *Instructions for Light Infantry and Riflemen*, produced by Beresford's ADC William Warre for the training of the Caçadores and published in Lisbon in 1810. (Courtesy R.J. Tennant)

RIGHT Lieutenant-Colonel Charles MacLeod commanded the 43rd in the Peninsula with the greatest distinction, notably when the Light Division was outposting the line of the river Coa. Described by Wellington as 'an ornament to his profession', McLeod was mortally wounded in the storming of the breaches at Badajoz. Sergeant Thomas Blood of his regiment declared that there was not a man in the 43rd 'but would have stood between him and the fatal ball... so esteemed was he by all.' Note that he wears epaulettes on top of barely visible shoulder wings, a practice of field-grade officers of light infantry.

A number of other 'foreign corps' were constituted and trained as light infantry, some more effective than others. Among the most exotically uniformed were the two corps of Greek Light Infantry employed in the Mediterranean theatre. An account of their participation in the attack on Santa Maura fort in March 1810 described how they 'no sooner came within the smell of powder than... they remained prone on their faces until the 35th passed them. This attachment to the soil, although an amiable feeling in some instances, is rather inconvenient in the case of storming a fort. The title of this regiment was evidently a misnomer; no troops could better deserve the name of *heavy* infantry than those who became altogether immovable.' (The official report of the action mentioned the cause of this as being 'the peculiar mode of fighting of the Greeks'.)[42]

Composite battalions

Composite battalions continued to be employed, notably the two flank battalions formed to increase the number of tactical units in Graham's army in the Barrosa campaign. One was commanded by the rifleman Sir Andrew Barnard (four companies of 3/95th, and the two flank companies of the 47th), the other by LtCol 'Mad John' Browne of the 28th (the flank companies from the l/9th, l/28th and 2/82nd). It was Browne's battalion that made the assault on the Cerro de Puerco at Barrosa to buy time for the rest of Graham's force to come up. Graham told him to advance in skirmish order but then changed his mind, telling Browne to 'close the men into a compact battalion'. 'That I will, with pleasure,' replied 'Mad John', 'for it is more in my way than light bobbing.'[43]

In the subsequent hopeless endeavour the battalion came under fire from three French battalions and eight guns, and suffered heavy losses before the survivors reverted to their light infantry training and took cover. Subsequently a wounded officer, Robert Blakeney of the 28th, gathered just eight or ten men (mainly from the 9th's grenadiers and his own light company) and took a run at a French howitzer. He captured it, and on looking round he found that more than a hundred men had left cover and followed him. Others joined at every step, enabling him to advance further and deflect a French attempt to reinforce their line elsewhere. This astonishing conduct was not influenced by the sight of success elsewhere, for the rest of the field was hidden from view, so it must have been the consequence of the initiative and determination fostered by light infantry training and morale.

Composite battalions formed from a brigade's light companies were used routinely in the Peninsula, their constitution later being detailed in a General Order dated 9 May 1815 at Brussels prior to the opening of the Waterloo campaign. The light companies of each brigade were to 'act together as a battalion of light infantry, under the command of a Field Officer or Captain, to be selected for the occasion by the General Officer commanding the brigade, upon all occasions on which the brigade may be formed in line or column, whether for a march or to oppose the enemy', but on all other occasions the light companies were to remain part of their own battalions.

One such light company was involved in a remarkable manoeuvre at Quatre Bras, that of the 44th, commanded by Lt Alexander Riddock. Surrounded by French cavalry and with no ammunition left, Riddock chose an audacious form of salvation: 'I instantly formed four deep and charged bayonets, the rear rank with ported arms, and fought my way through the French Cavalry until I reached the south side of the Square of my Regiment. But so hot and hard pressed was the Regiment on all sides, that I could obtain no admission, and my ammunition being gone we had no other alternative than lie down close to the Square, and crave their friendly protection.'[44]

G. LIGHT INFANTRY IN THE 'REVERSE SLOPE' TACTIC

The 'reverse slope' tactic, as employed most prominently by Wellington, was a most effective counter to the French system of attack that had proved so effective against other armies. An early example of this practice, at Vimeiro, was described by George Landmann: 'The 50th were in line, on the right of the reserve guns, and just sufficiently retired from the crest of the hill to be out of sight of the enemy; and instead of advancing in line, or by divisions or companies, to fire on the enemy, each man advanced singly when he had loaded, so as to see into the valley, and fired, on having taken his aim; he then fell back into his place to reload. By this management the enemy concluded that the guns were supported by a small number of Light Infantry only.' (See Landmann, in Select Bibliography; Vol II, pp.203–03.)

In this depiction of a notional but typical action, a French six-company battalion is advancing (**blue arrow**) with a frontage of two companies, each in three ranks, followed by two companies similarly in line and a fifth at the rear, while the sixth (voltigeur) company advances ahead in a skirmish screen to harass the enemy with its musketry. This columnar formation enabled an advance at speed without losing cohesion; but, as only the first two ranks could use their muskets, the column would deploy into line before contact with the enemy so as to bring more men into the firing line, and the preceding skirmishers would fall back to give them an uninterrupted field of fire.

The British counter to this tactic was to post a battalion behind the crest of a ridge, with just its light company deployed forward of the crest to exchange fire with the French skirmishers. With the main body thus concealed, the French were unable to gauge the moment for deploying into line. As they approached the crest, still in column, the British skirmishers would fall back round the flanks (**green arrows**), while the main British line advanced to the crest (**red arrows**), and, with every musket in nine companies brought to bear, devastated the head of the unsuspecting French column by volley-fire. Having shot down the head of the column, the British would execute a limited bayonet-charge which almost inevitably caused the French to break. Thereupon the British would halt and withdraw back over the crest to await another enemy attack, when the procedure could be repeated. Meanwhile the light company would have reassembled in two bodies behind the flanks of the line, and as the main body retired it would sally out once again to re-form the skirmish line.

(1) The British line, still hidden below the skyline but about to advance up to the crest, with the colour-party in the centre.
(2) The light company's skirmish line.
(3) The advancing French battalion, preceded by
(4) the skirmishers of its voltigeur company.
(5) The routes of the British light-company skirmishers as they retire to clear the front of their battalion, which then advances to contact, while
(6) the light company forms in two halves, ready to run forward again after the French withdrawal. The presence of the British skirmishers was thus crucial to the successful employment of this manoeuvre, in confusing the enemy about the size and location of the British line.

THE LIGHT DIVISION: ILLUSTRATIVE ACTIONS

Although the Light Division was an elite formation in the Peninsular army, little attempt was made to preserve them for the exercise of their particular skills; their ability to act equally well as conventional infantry led them to be used in such desperate endeavours as the storming of the breaches at Ciudad Rodrigo and Badajoz. In these bloody actions the sharpshooting skills of the covering parties of riflemen were highly effective, but otherwise the battalions suffered terrible casualties: for example, the losses of the principal battalions of the division (43rd, 52nd, and l/95th) in the storming of Badajoz numbered 58 officers and 871 other ranks, of whom 15 officers and 163 other ranks were killed.

William Napier of the 43rd was subsequently the author of the first great history of the Peninsular War. He received the Gold Medal for commanding his regiment at Salamanca, the Nivelle and Nive, and clasps to the Military General Service Medal for a further three actions. This shows the non-regulation pelisse worn by officers of the 43rd, and the CB awarded to Napier in June 1815. (Engraving after 'Miss Jones')

Mixed tactics: the Nivelle, 10 November 1813

The competence and flexibility of the light infantry were demonstrated in countless actions of the Peninsular War. One remarkable operation was the Light Division's attack on the Lesser Rhune and Mouiz fort at the battle of the Nivelle, by the brigades of Sir James Kempt (l/43rd, 1/ and 3/95th, 17th Portuguese) and John Colborne (l/52nd, 2/95th, 1st and 3rd Caçadores – though for this operation the 95th elements were exchanged between the two brigades). Defended by four battalions, the French position on the precipitous Lesser Rhune was an ascending triple row of stone walls styled, from front to rear, the Place d'Armes, Magpie's Nest, and at the top the Donjon ('keep').

This position was Kempt's target, and his brigade advanced in darkness. Sergeant-Major Russell of the 43rd flourished his sword in a theatrical gesture and called out 'England expects every man will this day do his duty; then follow me to victory!' British troops were rarely susceptible to oratory: this 'only excited a laugh of derision... but was not without inspiriting effect'. The brigade moved in silence to its advanced picquet line and lay down, John Maclean of the 43rd noting that the 95th under their white blankets resembled a flock of sheep in the darkness.

On the right, the 2/95th advanced in skirmish order and drove in the French picquets, and though further advance was blocked they achieved their purpose in keeping the French occupied, for the loss of only one rifleman killed. On the left, the main attack by William Napier's 43rd demonstrated the flexibility of the best light troops: two companies formed a skirmish line to keep the French busy, while the remaining eight advanced in column at a run to attack the French flank. Four companies then changed formation and dashed forward in line, the remaining four providing the first support and the 17th Portuguese the reserve. Joined by the two skirmishing companies, they scaled and overran the first lines, and as Napier began to reorganize them for the final push on the Donjon its garrison retired, under pressure from another flank attack led by Kempt together with Napier's four supporting companies and the 17th Portuguese. (One of the French officers, about to shoot a soldier of the 43rd, was brought down before he could fire when the man threw his bayoneted, unloaded musket like a javelin, impaled the officer through the thigh, and took him prisoner.)

The limits of discipline

While acknowledging the particular qualities of the light infantry as praised by Capt Hopkins of the 43rd (see page 38), we must not imagine that they were choirboys. A passage from John Cooper of the 7th Royal Fuzileers describes how his regiment's light-company skirmishers drove in a French picquet at Orthes:

'We directly surprised a picquet behind a farmhouse. They were busy cooking; but their bugler roused them, and they fell back, firing briskly... Our company was posted behind a large building, and commenced firing in rapid bo-peep fashion. Some of our men in the meantime broke into the house, and finding a store of wine, handed it out copiously to the combatants, so that the game was "Drink and Fire, Fire and Drink". Others were engaged in stoning and bagging the wandering, astonished poultry. Tired of inaction, Sergeant Simpson, who was wounded... on the heights of Pampeluna, shouted, "Come, let us charge these fellows!" Away he and most of the company went double quick, and drove the enemy from their hiding places; but poor Simpson received a shot which laid him dead.

'Receiving a reinforcement, the enemy drove our men back, and stripped our wounded of their knapsacks, etc... I was sent with a party to make a circuit farther to the left, in search of French skirmishers who might be skulking behind hedges, etc. In our road we came to a deserted farm house. My companions would enter for plunder. I warned them of their danger, and moved on. While they were rummaging the house, Lord Wellington and his staff passed; but being occupied with things of greater moment, he did not notice us.' (See Cooper, J.S., in Select Bibliography; pp.118–19.)

On the other part of the French position, the 1/ and 3/95th deployed in an extended skirmish screen to cover the l/52nd which outflanked the Mouiz fort, with the 1st and 3rd Caçadores in support. Snodgrass, commanding the 1st Caçadores, asked if his men could lead, because 'if the 52nd were to give way, I think the Caçadores will give way, too; but if [the 1st Caçadores] lead the attack, with the 52nd behind, it will be of no consequence if they give way or not.' Colborne knew his men: 'Make yourself quite easy; the 52nd will not give way.'[45] With the 95th keeping the French occupied, Colborne led the 52nd in column-of-threes around the flank and deployed in the rear of the French position – whereupon the defenders of the Mouiz position bolted, followed by the garrison of the Donjon. The speed, daring, and flexibility of these manoeuvres left the French 'perfectly thunderstruck' according to Harry Smith, and caused their complete demoralization.

The subsequent attack by Colborne upon an even stronger position, the Signals Redoubt, stalled at a huge ditch with heavy casualties, but, realizing their position was hopeless, the French defenders surrendered on condition that they would be taken prisoner by the 52nd and not by Spaniards. William Napier wrote bitterly of this stage of the operation, with the loss of 'two hundred soldiers of a regiment never surpassed in arms since arms were first borne by man'; but Harry Smith called the first stage 'the most beautiful attack ever made in the history of war', and it represented the pinnacle of light infantry capabilities.[46 & 47]

Skirmishing tactics: Tarbes, 20 March 1814

In contrast to this combination of conventional infantry formations with open order, at Tarbes an attack by the Light Division was mounted entirely in skirmishing mode. All three battalions of the 95th assaulted a steep, wooded hill held by a French brigade; they appear to have advanced in skirmish order and in echelon, each with three companies in the front line and the remainder in reserve, using available cover. William Napier surmised that the French mistook the 95th for Portuguese because of their dark uniforms, and so counter-attacked 'muzzle to muzzle' with extreme ferocity. Having swept away the French skirmishers, the 95th compelled the remainder to retire (though French sources claimed this was caused by a threat to their flank). In this operation, so unusual in that it was mounted entirely by skirmishers, the 95th lost 11 officers and 80 other ranks, but inflicted casualties entirely out of proportion. George Simmons wrote that 'I never saw Frenchmen before so thick on the ground; it was covered with dead bodies.' Harry Smith recalled that 'Three successive times the enemy, with greatly superior force, endeavoured to drive them off a hill, but the loss of the enemy from the fire of our Rifles was so great that one could not believe one's eyes. I certainly had never seen the dead lie so thick, nor ever did, except subsequently at Waterloo.' So unusual was the sight that Wellington himself was urged to view it; he replied that 'I require no novel proof of the destructive fire of your rifles.'[48]

This action provided a touching example of the bond between officers and other ranks; when George Simmons was brought down with a shot in the knee his soldier-servant Henry Short ran up 'and, with an oath, observed, "You shall not hit him again but through my body," and deliberately placed himself in front of me'.[49]

John Colborne, later Field-Marshal Lord Seaton (1778–1863), portrayed as lieutenant-colonel of the 52nd Light Infantry which he commanded in the Peninsula and at Waterloo. George Napier claimed that 'except the Duke of Wellington, I know no officer in the British army his equal'; and that Colborne possessed the qualities vital for a commander of light infantry – 'with the most intrepid bravery, a coolness of head... nothing can take him by surprise or flurry him.'

Flexible tactics: Waterloo, 18 June 1815

A final example of the flexibility of formation was provided by the counter-attack of Adam's Brigade against the advancing Imperial Guard at Waterloo, initiated by John Colborne of the 52nd. The entire brigade comprised light infantry, including also the 71st, 2/95th, and two companies of the 3/95th.

An unusually strong battalion (the Waterloo 'morning state' listed 59 officers and 1,108 other ranks), the 52nd had formed two squares, and was ordered to fall back as the French approached. This Colborne did, in two lines according to his own account, but realizing 'the necessity of menacing the flank of the French Columns', he formed a line 'nearly parallel with the

H **BRIGADE ATTACK**
This plate illustrates a notional attack mounted by a light infantry brigade, showing tactical features similar to those described in the text for the action by Kempt's and Colborne's brigades at the battle of the Nivelle (pages 54–55). The scene imagines a wooded position on high ground held by a French brigade, with elements sheltered by the woodland and a strong screen of skirmishers at the front of their position (1).

The British attack is preceded by two companies of light infantry in extended order (2), advancing to engage the French skirmishers, with their company reserves (3) held back behind the skirmish line. On each flank of the light infantry is a company of Rifles (4), also in extended order, and also with their company reserves (5).

Following the two-company skirmish line in the centre of the British position is the principal assault force, four companies of light infantry (6) in two-deep line in close order. The reserve of the light infantry battalion is provided by its remaining four companies (7), in quarter-distance column. From this position they can second the assault, or cover its withdrawal if the attack fails, allowing the retreating assault companies to rally and re-form behind the reserve. On each flank of the main position is a company of Rifles (8), in skirmish line with a reserve, to protect the flanks and to be available to execute a flanking movement against the French position. As a brigade reserve, a battalion of five companies of Portuguese Caçadores (9) is stationed at the rear. The brigade commander's group have taken up position on a hill (10), where a chapel offers a vantage point.

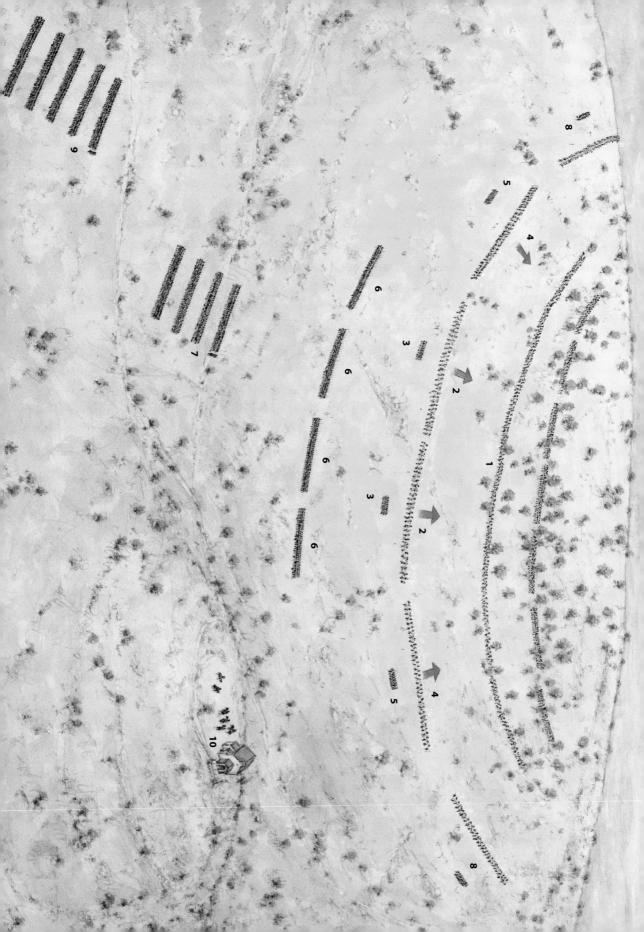

The 52nd prepares to make its decisive move against the advancing Imperial Guard at Waterloo. At right are an officer and private of the 2/95th Rifles, a battalion adjacent to the 52nd in this action. (Engraving by S. Mitan after George Jones)

moving Columns of the French Imperial Guards. I ordered a strong Company to extend in our front [and] ordered the extended Company of the 52nd, about 100 men, under the command of Lieutenant [Mathew] Anderson, to advance as quickly as possible without any support except from the Battalion, and to fire into the French Column at any distance. Thus the 52nd formed in two lines of half Companies, the rear line at 10 paces distant from the front... Three or four Companies of the 95th were formed on our left rather to the rear of our line.' Presumably in expectation of meeting the French attack, the 2/95th had changed formation to one not normally associated with them, as 1st Lt John Budgen recalled: 'a very short period (say less than half an hour) before the last advance of the Enemy, our line was formed four deep, our formation having previously been two deep as usual.' The four-deep formation was also adopted by the 71st, but it was some time before they advanced. Lieutenant George Gawler of the 52nd described the encounter:

'So close was the left Company to the Imperial Column that it was compelled to wheel back on its right, while the rest of the Regiment came forward on their left. The Enemy was pressing on with shouts, which rose above the noise of the firing, and his fire was so intense that, with but half the ordinary length of front [because they were four deep] *at least* 150 of the 52nd fell in less than four minutes. I almost think in less than three, for there was not the slightest check of the right flank below the average of the old wheeling time. When the 52nd was nearly parallel to the Enemy's flank, Sir J. Colborne gave the word "Charge, charge". It was answered from the Regiment by a loud steady cheer and a hurried dash to the front. In the next ten seconds the Imperial Guard, broken into the wildest confusion, and scarcely firing a shot to cover its retreat, was rushing towards the hollow road in the rear of La Haye Sainte'.[50]

The ability to change formation, and to sustain such casualties without pausing, was further evidence of the remarkable training and morale of the best light infantry.

AFTERMATH

Perhaps as in the period after the American War of Independence, some believed that the light infantry skills perfected in the Peninsula became diluted in the years that followed. Harry Smith claimed that the success of the squares at Waterloo 'has destroyed the field movement... All that light-troop duty which [Moore] taught, by which the world through the medium of the Spanish War was saved, is now replaced by the most heavy of manoeuvres, by squares, centre formations, and moving in masses... all because the Prussians and Russians did not know how to move quicker, we, forsooth, must adopt their ways.'[51]

Perhaps something not dissimilar was reported by Lord Mark Kerr in 1865 when commanding the 13th Light Infantry; an expert in light infantry duty, he had led it with skill in the Crimea and Indian Mutiny. He was told by Gen Sir John Pennefather, 'You have ruined my field day entirely by sending out your skirmishers so far to the front. I never send mine out more than 20 paces in front of the line' – 'and this', commented Lord Mark, 'from a General who was in the Crimea, and is now commanding the Camp of Instruction.'[52]

In the post-Waterloo period the distinction between light and conventional infantry certainly declined markedly, with the skills traditionally attributed to light troops being incorporated into the ordinary infantry training. Moreover, the general introduction of the Minie rifle before the Crimean War meant that the light infantry distinction became more a matter of *esprit de corps* than tactical difference, a development increased by the very nature of the colonial warfare that dominated the later 19th century. The essence of Moore's light infantry and its entire ethos in effect formed the foundations of general infantry service, as it does to the present day.

When a centenary dinner was held in June 1908 to commemorate the formation of the Light Division, the Duke of Connaught's address quoted William Napier on the light infantry: 'Six years of warfare could not detect a flaw in their system, nor were they ever matched in courage and skill. Those three regiments [43rd, 52nd, 95th] were avowedly the best that England ever had under arms. This is no idle boast. War was better known, the art more advanced under Napoleon than in any age of the world before, and the French veterans – those victors of a thousand battles – never could stand before my gallant men'.[53]

The 71st (Highland) Light Infantry at Waterloo, where they served in Adam's Brigade. During the final advance of the Imperial Guard they were on the right and to the rear of the 52nd. This regiment was unique in retaining aspects of its previous Highland uniform; the diced bonnet was blocked into the shape of a shako, the officers wore Highland sashes, and the pipers were retained. (Engraving by S. Mitan after George Jones)

SELECT BIBLIOGRAPHY

Beaufoy, Capt H., *Scloppetaria: or Considerations on the Nature and Use of Rifled Barrel Guns*, written under the *nom-de-plume* 'A Corporal of Riflemen' (London, 1808)

Blackmore, H.L., *British Military Firearms 1650–1850* (London, 1961)

Butler, LtCol L., *The Annals of the King's Royal Rifle Corps* (London, 1913–23; Vol I 'The Royal Americans', Vol II 'The Green Jacket'; Appendix dealing with Uniforms, Arms and Equipment by S.M. Milne & MajGen A. Terry (London, 1913)

Caldwell, G.J., & Cooper, R.B.E., *Rifle Green in the Peninsula*, 4 vols (Great Glen, Leicestershire, 1998–2015)

Cooke, J.H., *Memoir of the Late War: A Personal Narrative of Captain J.H. Cooke, 43rd Light Infantry* (London, 1831)

Cooke, J.H., *Narrative of Events in the South of France, and of the Attack on New Orleans in 1814 and 1815* (London, 1835)

Cooper, J.S., *Rough Notes of Seven Campaigns in Portugal, Spain, France and America* (Carlisle, 1914; orig pub 1869)

Cooper, Capt T.H., *A Practical Guide for the Light Infantry Officer* (London, 1806)

Cope, Sir William, Bt, *History of the Rifle Brigade (The Prince Consort's Own, formerly the 95th)* (London, 1877)

Craufurd, MajGen R., *Standing Orders, as given out and enforced by the late Major-Gen. Robt. Craufurd, for the Use of the Light Division* (London, 1814)

Fuller, MajGen J.F.C., *Sir John Moore's System of Training* (London, 1924)

Fuller, MajGen J.F.C., *British Light Infantry in the Eighteenth Century* (London, 1925)

Fuller, MajGen J.F.C., 'Sir John Moore's Light Infantry Instructions of 1798–1799' in *Journal of the Society for Army Historical Research*, Vol XXX (1952) pp. 68–75

Gates, D., *The British Light Infantry Arm c.1790–1815* (London, 1987)

Glover, R., *Peninsular Preparation: The Reform of the British Army 1795–1809* (Cambridge, 1963)

Gross, Baron, *Duties of an Officer in the Field and Principally of Light Troops* (London, 1801)

Haythornthwaite, P.J., *The Armies of Wellington* (London, 1994)

Haythornthwaite, P.J., *Napoleonic Weapons and Warfare: Napoleonic Infantry* (London, 2001)

Haythornthwaite, P.J., *British Rifleman 1797–1815*, Osprey Warrior 47 (Oxford, 2002)

Haythornthwaite, P.J., *British Napoleonic Infantry Tactics 1792–1815*, Osprey Elite 164 (Oxford, 2008)

Kincaid, Sir John, *Adventures in the Rifle Brigade* (London, 1830)

Kincaid, Sir John, *Random Shots from a Rifleman* (London, 1835)

Landmann, Col G., *Recollections of My Military Life* (London, 1854)

Levinge, Sir R.G.A., Bt, *Historical Records of the Forty-Third Regiment* (London, 1868)

Manningham, Col Coote, *Military Lectures delivered to the Officers of the 95th (Rifle) Regiment at Shorn-Cliffe Barracks, Kent, during the Spring of 1803* (London, 1803; r/p with intro by Col W. Verner, 1897)

Mitchell, Col J., *Thoughts on Tactics and Military Organisation* (London, 1838)

Moorsom, W.S., *Historical Record of the 52nd Regiment (Oxfordshire Light Infantry) from the Year 1755 to the Year 1858* (London, 1860)

Nafziger, G.F., *Imperial Bayonets: Tactics of the Napoleonic Battery, Battalion and Brigade as Found in Contemporary Regulations* (London & Mechanicsburg, 1996)

Newbolt, Sir Henry, *The Story of the Oxfordshire and Buckinghamshire Light Infantry* (London, 1915)

Nosworthy, B., *Battle Tactics of Napoleon and his Enemies* (London, 1995)

Oman, Carola, *Sir John Moore* (London, 1953)

Oman, Sir Charles, *A History of the Peninsular War* (Oxford, 1902–30)

Rigaud, MajGen G., *Celer et Audax: A Sketch of the Services of the Fifth Battalion Sixtieth Regiment (Rifles)* (Oxford, 1879)

Rottenburg, F. de, *Regulations for the Exercise of Riflemen and Light Infantry, and Instructions for their Conduct in the Field* (London, 1799)

Strachan, H., *From Waterloo to Balaclava: Tactics, Technology, and the British Army, 1815–1854* (Cambridge, 1985)

Verner, W., *History and Campaigns of the Rifle Brigade* (London, 1905–13)

SOURCE NOTES

(1) Patterson, J., *A Series of Original Portraits and Character Etchings* (Edinburgh; John Kay, 1838) Vol II, p. 44

(2) *British Military Library or Journal* (London, 1801) Vol II, p. 112

(3) Stewart of Garth, Col D., *Sketches of the Character, Manners and Present State of the Highlanders of Scotland* (Edinburgh, 1822) Vol I, p. 444

(4) *British Military Library or Journal* (London, 1801) Vol II, p. 106

(5) Moore, J.C., *The Life of Lieut. General Sir John Moore KCB* (London, 1834) Vol II, p. 5

(6) *Journal of the Society for Army Historical Research* (1952) Vol XXX, p. 70

(7) Quoted in Fuller, J.F.C., *Sir John Moore's System of Training* (London, 1924) pp. 69–70

(8) Brownrigg, B., *The Life and Letters of Sir John Moore* (Oxford, 1922) p. 142

(9) *United Service Magazine* (1842) Vol II, pp. 83–85

(10) *Colburn's United Service Magazine* (1846) Vol III, p. 563

(11) *United Service Journal* (1829) Vol II, pp. 208–09. The reference was to Gen Sir Ralph Abercombie (1734–1801), the widely admired commander who was mortally wounded at Alexandria.

(12) Wilson, Sir Robert, *Enquiry into the Present State of the Military Forces of the British Empire* (London, 1804) p. 68

(13) *Colburn's United Service Magazine* (1844) Vol III, pp. 276–77

(14) ibid (1845) Vol I, p. 447

(15) Kincaid, Sir John, *Random Shots from a Rifleman* (London, 1835); 1908 combined edn with *Adventures in the Rifle Brigade* (London, 1830), p. 253

(16) Napier, Sir George, *Passages in the Early Military Life of General Sir George T. Napier*, ed. Gen W.C.E. Napier (London, 1884) pp. 47–48

(17) Leach, J., *Rough Sketches in the Life of an Old Soldier* (London, 1831) p. 262

(18) Harris, B.R., *The Recollections of Rifleman Harris*, ed. H. Curling (London, 1848; r/p, ed. C. Hibbert, London, 1970), pp. 92–93, 102

(19) Fuller, op cit, p. 163

(20) *Oxfordshire Light Infantry Chronicle* (1901) p. 162

(21) Gross, Baron, *Duties of an Officer in the Field, and Principally of Light Troops* (London, 1801) pp. vii–viii

(22) G. Napier, op cit, pp. 13–14

(23) Anon, *A Manual for Volunteer Corps of Infantry* (London, 1803) p. 32

(24) *Colburn's United Service Magazine* (1845) Vol I, pp. 446–47

(25) *United Service Journal* (1841) Vol I, p. 472

(26) ibid (1829) Vol II, p. 578

(27) Manningham, C., *Military Lectures delivered to the Officers of the 95th Rifle Regiment* (London, 1803, r/p 1897) p. 44

(28) Napier, W.F.P., *The Life and Opinions of General Sir Charles James Napier GCB* (London, 1857) Vol I, pp. 59–60

(29) anon, ed. A.J. Gans, *The Diary of a British Soldier, May 5, 1793 to March 4, 1795* (San Francisco, 1941) p. 41

(30) Napier, W.F.P., *History of the War in the Peninsula and in the South of France from the Year 1807 to the Year 1814* (London, 1828–40) Vol I, p. 458

(31) *United Service Journal* (1840) Vol I, p. 223

(32) *Colburn's United Service Magazine* (1844) Vol III, p. 231

(33) *United Service Magazine* (1842) Vol II, p. 84

(34) Landmann, Col G., *Recollections of My Military Life* (London, 1854) Vol II, pp. 293–95

(35) *Colburn's United Service Magazine* (1845) Vol I, p. 89

(36) ibid (1844) Vol III, pp. 279–80

(37) ibid, p. 276

(38) ibid, pp.52–53

(39) *United Service Journal* (1840) Vol I, p. 362

(40) *Colburn's United Service Magazine* (1844) Vol II, p. 110

(41) Warre, Sir William, ed. Revd E. Warre, *Letters from the Peninsula 1808–1812* (London, 1909) p. 97

(42) *United Service Journal* (1840) Vol III, p. 331; *London Gazette,* 23 June 1810

(43) Blakeney, R., ed. J. Sturgis, *A Boy in the Peninsular War* (London, 1899) p. 187

(44) Siborne, H.T., *The Waterloo Letters* (London, 1891) p. 381

(45) Moore Smith, G.C., *The Life of John Colborne, Field-Marshal Lord Seaton* (London, 1903) p. 192

(46) Napier, W.P.F., *History...,* Vol VI, p. 359

(47) Smith, Sir Harry, ed. G.C. Moore Smith, *The Autobiography of Sir Harry Smith* (London, 1902) p. 146

(48) ibid, pp. 174–75

(49) Simmons, G., ed. W. Verner, *A British Rifle Man* (London, 1899) p. 341

(50) H.T. Siborne, op cit, pp. 284, 293, 299–300

(51) Smith, op cit, p. 278

(52) Everett, MajGen Sir Henry, *The History of the Somerset Light Infantry (Prince Albert's) 1685–1914* (London, 1934) p. 265

(53) *Oxfordshire Light Infantry Chronicle* (1908) p. 113

INDEX